**DON'T MISS ANY OF THE FABULOUS SECRETS
REVEALED IN THIS
UNIQUE PARTY-GIVER'S HANDBOOK**

FIND OUT THE INSIDE SCOOP ON HOW TO

- Order a genuine Mardi Gras King Cake
- Buy a life-size cutout of Marilyn Monroe, Albert Einstein, or Darth Vader
- Send for ludicrous game prizes for a Nerd Party
- Make a flapper dress for less than twenty dollars
- Transform your living room into the Casbah
- Find a hilarious "horse's ass" trophy
- Write totally tasteless, exceptionally funny signs for a Politically Incorrect Party
- Barter for "treasures" in your own Middle Eastern bazaar
- Immortalize your party in a way guests will love!

. . . AND MORE!

Other possible ideas
- Create "tip sheets" for an Oscar Night competition
- Test your geek perception with the Nerd Quiz
- Try your hand at group limericks

Rock the Casbah

The Complete Guide to Hosting Your Own Theme Party

by Ellen Hoffman

Illustrations by Louise Farrell

A DELL TRADE PAPERBACK

A DELL TRADE PAPERBACK

Published by
Dell Publishing
a division of
Bantam Doubleday Dell Publishing Group, Inc.
1540 Broadway
New York, New York 10036

Library of Congress Cataloging in Publication Data

Hoffman, Ellen (Ellen N.)
    Rock the Casbah : the complete guide to hosting your own theme party / by Ellen Hoffman ; illustrations by Louise Farrell.
        p.   cm.
    Includes bibliographical references.
    ISBN 0-440-50608-5
    1. Entertaining. I. Title.
GV1471.H62   1996
792.3—dc20   95-30131
                                                                                                      CIP

Printed in the United States of America

Published simultaneously in Canada

April 1996

10 9 8 7 6 5 4 3 2 1

FFG

For Ken, who makes me want to party

With special thanks to Pat, for getting this project off the ground; to "Mr. Oscar," partygoer extraordinaire, whose original Nerd Quiz and Oscar tip sheets have been memorialized in this book; to Ken, for all those late nights; to the entire New Year's Eve group, for showing that we're never too old to party; and to my parents, for being good sports even though they don't always understand why I do the things I do.

The thing about parties is, once you start,
you just want more.
—*Andy Warhol's Party Book*

Contents

PREFACE

Rock the Casbah: The Complete Guide to Hosting Your Own Theme Party presents some offbeat—and we hope entertaining—alternatives to your run-of-the-mill cocktail party. The soirees described here have been thoroughly tested by a group of "baby boomers" who, for more than ten years, have participated in a wide variety of theme parties—from A Night in the Casbah to '60s TV. The beauty of these parties is that they cost very little, stretch the limits of your imagination, and are as much fun to plan as to attend. The parties we have thrown have ranged in size from six to sixty. While some required months of planning, others were conceived and executed within days.

What we present here are really the basics for throwing your own theme parties. You can make them as simple or elaborate as you wish. Some people may want to follow our ideas verbatim, while others may wish to use our suggestions as a jumping-off point for more creative ventures.

We hope that the tales of our partying adventures—and mis-adventures—will inspire you to give it a try. There is a lot to be said for taking a trip to the joke shop, putting on a silly costume and dancing shoes, and spending an evening partying with good friends.

INTRODUCTION

*H*ow does a tradition of great partying begin? In our case, it dates back to December 1982. As New Year's Eve rapidly approached, we realized that we hadn't received one invitation. As it turned out, neither had our downstairs neighbors. So the four of us were sitting around our dining-room table with a bottle of wine, trying to think creatively about how best to salvage this misfortune. What we came up with—not surprisingly for a cold December night in Boston—was the idea of creating our own party around the theme of a trip to Hawaii. We were not in the least put off by the fact that none of us had ever been there.

We needed very little: beachwear, leis, tropical drinks, and, of course, a Don Ho album. Any extras—Groucho glasses with a beach hat, a hula costume made from a pair of old curtains, and a two-foot plaster bust of Elvis (with appropriate beach apparel)—were added spontaneously. What resulted was one of the best New Year's Eves of our lives—and we never looked back.

As the years go by, we are becoming more sophisticated. But some things remain constant: Our best props cost next to nothing and come from thrift stores and tacky joke shops, our costumes are always ridiculous, and we have a fantastic time. The themes always guarantee a lot of laughs. Most important, the plaster Elvis has become a party mascot—and always comes dressed for the occasion!

The following are twelve suggestions for throwing your own theme parties. I've included information on setting up the parties, costumes, prizes, activities—but like any successful soiree, your party will soon take on a life of its own.

No two parties will be the same. Your guests will create their own characters, who, in turn, will define many of the interactions. Don't be rigid about following a special format. Sometimes planned activities will never take place, and that's okay. If everyone is having fun, don't over-orchestrate. Spontaneity will make your party a success. Marilyn Monroe may end up dancing with Janis Joplin, Fred Astaire with Tina Turner, or Elizabeth Taylor with Fidel Castro.

The most important thing is to encourage your guests to get into the spirit. Remember: All is fair in love and war . . . and theme parties!

Twelve Theme Parties

1. Wagons Ho (or Shootout at the O.K. Corral)
2. A Night in the Casbah (or Midnight at the Oasis)
3. The Speakeasy
4. The Politically Incorrect Party
5. Faded Fads
6. Great Entertainers
7. The Nerd Party
8. The Watergate Party
9. The Scandals Party
10. '50s/'60s/'70s TV
11. The Cold War Party
12. Oscar Night: A Party in Two Parts

WAGONS HO

(OR SHOOTOUT AT THE O.K. CORRAL)

If you have never thrown a theme party, the Wagons Ho Party is a good introduction. To get in the mood, and for some great ideas, get a copy of *Way Out West* by Jane and Michael Stern (HarperCollins, 1993), which will be sure to provide inspiration.

Costuming is easy: a Western shirt with bandanna, a denim skirt, checked blouse, vest, and, of course, the traditional cowboy hat. For those who wish to look like authentic cowboys, buy shaggy bathroom rugs, attach them to a belt, and faster than you can lasso a doggie, you have a nice pair of chaps. (See illustration.)

Some of the more creative guests may wish to come as specific characters from history or television: Wild Bill Hickok; Annie Oakley; Roy Rogers and Dale Evans; one of the Cartwright boys from *Bonanza*; Paladin from *Have Gun Will Travel*; Miss Kitty, Chester, or Marshal Dillon from *Gunsmoke*; Buffalo Bill; McCabe and Mrs. Miller; or even Butch Cassidy with members of the Hole in the Wall Gang. If you think you could pass as a young Clint

Eastwood, consider coming as Rowdy Yates from *Rawhide*. If you have a sadistic streak, think of coming as Little Bill, the tough lawman from *Unforgiven*.

For those who prefer a more generic character, consider coming as a dancehall girl, the saloonkeeper (complete with sleeve guards), the local preacher, the schoolmarm, the sheriff, a Pinkerton, a cowhand, a rodeo rider, or the camp cook.

INVITATIONS

How about sending out "Wanted" posters:

These could be rolled up and tied with a rawhide shoelace or a bandanna, and sent in mailing tubes.

If you are looking for something simpler, just use some of the dozens of Western motif stamps available. (See pages 129–30.) Seal the invitations with Western-style stickers.

Has your party calendar become too predictable?

Are you getting a little bored with the same old Christmas–New Year's–July 4th–Halloween routine? If so, consider celebrating some other "noteworthy" occasions.

FOOD

The menu should be based around ribs, corn bread, chili, beans, beans, and more beans. (Consider cheating by ordering out.) Outdoor parties could be cookouts.

Backdrop for Wagons Ho Party.
See instructions on page 132.

JANUARY

January 16—National Nothing Day

Maybe you're tired of partying after Christmas and New Year's Eve, but what better event to lift you out of the postholiday doldrums than a small get-together to celebrate National Nothing Day? Created by newspaperman Harold Pullman Coffin, this holiday—or nonholiday—was first observed in 1973.

DECOR

If it is warm weather and you have a backyard, this party lends itself to an outdoor barbecue. If possible, think about renting or bor-
rowing a horse from a farm or stable.

Because we had our Wagons Ho Party in an apartment in the
midst of a Boston winter, we were forced to depend on our trusty
backdrop, handmade swinging saloon doors, and imaginations to
set the mood.

For extra touches, we added a faux horse, Trigger, a sawhorse
with a head crafted from poster board and the mane and tail from
a mop. (See illustration.) If you want Trigger to be an authentic
stallion instead of a gelding, add Styrofoam balls (available from
trimming stores) or balloons and a candle. (We used a fabric candle that in real life is a Christmas tree ornament.)

Tables were set with red-and-white checked tablecloths.
(Plastic is fine.) Assorted plastic cowboys and Indians, as well
as snakes and desert creatures were added. Cacti (or quasi-
Western-looking plants from around the house) also can be placed
around the room. If you don't have any real cacti, do what we
did and create your own out of green poster or foam board
with toothpicks added as cactus needles. If you haven't vacu-
umed for a while, use the scattered "dust bunnies" as tumble-
weed.

If your time is limited, or you don't feel particularly creative,
there is no shame in buying prepared decorations. (See pages

134–35.) In fact, Western decorating kits, cowboy hats, and even a four-and-a-half-foot cactus are all readily available.

Elvis, as always, came appropriately dressed, wearing a small red plastic cowboy hat (intended for a children's party) and a very stunning red bandanna.

GAMES

If the party is outdoors, a horseshoe-throwing competition would be in order. If it's indoors, you could do the same in a miniature version. (Use freestanding paper towel racks as the posts, and old 45 records or Frisbee rings as horseshoes.)

January 30—The Beatles' Last Public Appearance

Celebrate this nostalgic event with a Beatles' Party. The last show took place on the roof of the Beatles' Apple Studios in London but was interrupted when police received complaints from neighbors. If you live in a warmer climate, think about re-creating the event as a roof party. Northerners could consider a roof backdrop of London to set the mood.

Customize a standard Pin the Tail on the Donkey game. Think about naming the donkey after one of your more ornery guests.

You might consider a Western TV trivia contest. Subjects could include naming the cowboy's/cowgirl's horse or identifying the theme songs from the shows. (See the music recommendations later in this chapter.)

For the outdoor party, think about Castrate the Bull (or pony). Make a life-size cardboard cutout of the animal, and attach Styrofoam balls (the kind used to make Christmas ornaments) at the correct anatomical location. Then fill a watergun with colored water. (Any old food dye will do.) Have your guests take turns "shooting off" the balls. The colored water will show who got closest. The best shot wins.

Depending on how rowdy you want to get, you may consider a Lasso Trigger game, where your guests take turns trying to lasso the faux horse (the very same animal that has just been humiliated in the Castrate the Pony game).

MUSIC

Stay with the country theme until you are ready for serious dancing. Consider the theme from *Rawhide, Zorro, Bonanza, Wagon Train,* or *Have Gun Will Travel*; "The Man Who Shot Liberty Valance" by Gene Pitney; "Ballad of the Alamo" by Marty Robbins or Bud and Travis; "Yellow Rose of Texas" by Mitch Miller; "Ragtime Cowboy Joe" by the Chipmunks; "Please Mr. Custer" by Larry Verne; or any recording by the Austin Outlaws, Gene

FEBRUARY

February 3—Halfway Point of Winter

Look in the *Farmer's Almanac* for the exact time (to the minute) and celebrate it as you would New Year's Eve. Party hats, blowers, and noisemakers would all be appropriate. A spring motif would also be suitable.

Autry, Patsy Cline, Sleepy LaBeef, Frankie Laine, Bill Monroe, Willie Nelson, Jimmie Rodgers, Roy Rogers, Texas Tornados, Jerry Jeff Walker, or Hank Williams.

Some "best-bet" tapes and CDs include:

- *The Best of Roy Rogers* (Curb Records). *Note:* Don't get too excited—"Happy Trails" isn't included.
- *Roy Rogers' Country Music Hall of Fame Series.*
- *Roy Rogers Tribute,* with numerous guest artists and such show-stoppers as "That's How the West Was Swung," and "Tumbling Tumbleweeds."
- *Sons of the Pioneers: Songs of the Train,* for such cuts as "Don't Fence Me In" and "Columbus Stockade Blues."
- Any of the Riders in the Sky's CDs, including *Best of the West Rides Again, Weeds and Water, Harmony Ranch, Cowboy Jubilee,* or *The Cowboy Way* (Rounder Records).
- One of the Songs of the West Series (Rhino), including *Volume 1, Cowboy Classics; Volume 2, Silver Screen Cowboys; Volume 3, Gene Autry and Roy Rogers;* and *Volume 4, Movie and Television Themes.*

PRIZES

Any of the above-mentioned tapes would be an appropriate prize.

If you like to bake (or don't mind a gallop to the local bakery), consider a nice basket of "buffalo chip" (chocolate) cookies: See

---

February 3—The Day the Music Died

Another idea for the same day is a memorial party to honor Buddy Holly, J. P. Richardson (better known as the Big Bopper), and Ritchie Valens, three rock 'n' roll legends who died in a plane crash on this day in 1959. Don McLean's recording of "American Pie" is a must. For a more subdued remembrance, you could make a big batch of popcorn and rent *The Buddy Holly Story.*

who's willing to take a bite. They can be presented in a plastic cowboy hat or wrapped in a bandanna.

We found a great "Horse's Ass" trophy at our local trophy store (Mission Trophy, 455 Massachusetts Avenue, Arlington Centre, MA 02174 [617] 648-7589). It is literally a small trophy that has a gold horse's rear end mounted on a marble pedestal. Period. A customized inscription could be added. Our store does the honors while you wait, but it pays to call ahead on this one.

A standard marksmanship trophy should be awarded to the winner of the Castrate the Bull (or pony) contest.

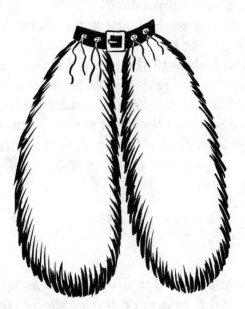

Bathroom rugs, attached to a belt, can give you a nice pair of chaps

---

February 3—Dan Quayle's Birthday

On this date in 1947, Dan Quayle was brought into the world. The possibilities for recognizing this event are limitless. If, however, like our former vice president, you somehow find yourself at a loss, consult back issues of *The Quayle Quarterly*.

Helpful Hint

Role Play Before the Party— But Keep the Blinds Drawn

Part of the fun of getting ready for a theme party is buying your costumes and then role playing to ensure you are comfortable in your part.

Before our Wagons Ho Party, we went out to a local toy store and bought holsters, six-shooters, and hats. When we got home, we couldn't wait to try on our gear. We ripped open our shopping bags, quickly donned our new purchases, and found ourselves in a spontaneous shootout. Satisfied that our props worked, we put them away.

Later that week, we were invited to an open house at a neighbor's home. Our host introduced us to another neighbor, a man who lived in the apartment building across the street from us. I began the conversation by saying that we lived on the third floor. "I know," he said. "I saw your shootout."

RE-CREATING WILSON FROM SHANE

The week before our Wagons Ho Party, we watched the video of *Shane* to get in the mood. For those unfamiliar with this 1953 classic, Alan Ladd plays Shane, the too-good-to-be-true reformed gunslinger. Jack Palance plays the archvillain Wilson, a gunfighter hired by the local cattle baron to get rid of the homesteaders—one way or the other.

A friend and I both decided to come as Wilson. The basic costume was sinister: black cowboy hat, vest, boots, dark brown pants, and a single leather glove. One essential part of the costume was a pair of spurs, necessary because when the quiet falls before the big showdown, you can hear the spurs jingling on the wooden planks of the two-bit Western town.

I was thrilled to find the last pair of spurs at the local toy store, and mentioned this to our friend—who wanted to be a more authentic Wilson. I knew that he was not having any luck finding spurs and that he—the ultimate bargain shopper—was not prepared to spend megabucks to buy real ones at a riding shop.

On the night of the party, the two Wilsons appeared—both with spurs! I was shocked. But on closer examination, I saw that our friend's spurs were not spurs at all, but pie trimmers wired onto his boots. He then confessed that, in frustration, he had gone to a hardware store looking for any kitchen utensil that could pass as spurs. He saw the pie trimmers and knew they were the best he'd do. The salesman commented, "You must be making a lot of pies."

A Night in the Casbah

or Midnight at the Oasis

This has the potential to be one of your more exotic theme parties because there is always a little mystery involved in a trip to the Casbah. To get in the mood, read *Arabian Nights* or rent the video of either *Casablanca* or *Algiers*.

Heighten the excitement of the evening by incorporating a voyage to North Africa into the party. For the first part of our Casbah Party, we came as assorted characters from all over the world traveling together on a ship bound for Morocco. Passengers included a Russian princess, a Texas millionaire, a Hassidic gem merchant, a sheik, members of the British royal family, and a Western newspaperman and his sexy companion.

At midnight, the boat docked. In reality, we all disappeared to different rooms to change costumes. (Everyone is told in advance to bring a second costume for the Casbah.) The Texas oilman re-emerged as the local leper, the Hassidic gem merchant was transformed into a bejeweled Muslim woman, and the newspaperman and his alluring companion became kvetchy American tourists who, to their horror, were constantly followed by the leper.

INVITATIONS

Think about buying (or making) miniplastic bags and filling them with exotic-smelling spices (paprika, cumin, curry powder, mustard seed, etc.). Staple the packets onto the front of the invitation and write: "Put a little spice in your life: Spend a Night in the Casbah."

A variation would be to write the invitation on a colored card, and place the card and the spices into a clear sandwich bag, which you fold over to be envelope size. Then place address labels on the plastic bag and place the stamp directly on the bag.

Helpful hint: If you are using plastic, send a few "test sample" invitations to yourself (or a friend) to see if they will make it through the U.S. Postal Service intact. Of most importance, make sure you use strong glue on the stamps because they tend to fall off in the mail.

DECOR

When guests arrive, the house should be dark, except for the room used as the boat. This room should be dimly lit with candles or flashlights.

February 6—Accession of Queen Elizabeth II

On February 6, 1952, Queen Elizabeth II assumed the throne upon the death of her father, King George VI. This is a perfect excuse for an Anglophile Party, where everyone could come as dukes and duchesses. It is also a great date for a Royal Scandals Party. If you're tired of Fergie and Andrew and Di and Charles, you can always come as the queen's Welsh corgies.

At midnight, when "the boat docks," subtle lighting (candles or flashlights and lamps draped with colored scarves) is turned on in the living room (or whichever room is used as the Casbah). The backdrop is hung on one of the walls, and the rest of the room can be liberally draped with fabric (bought at a local discount fabric store, of course) or sheets.

This would also be a wonderful setting for your all-purpose palm trees. (See page 134.) If available, a stuffed camel (of any size) should be added.

COSTUMES

This party offers a wide range of costume possibilities. The easiest—for both men and women—is to create a jellaba (a floor-length, hooded outer garment worn over street clothes for dust protection). A maroon fez (traditionally worn by men—but who is traditional?) is a nice addition. If you don't happen to have a fez (available in the Grand Bazaar in Istanbul for about $1—after bargaining), try wearing a round plant basket upside down. For authenticity, attach a black tassel to the top.

Okay, so much for the "safe" costumes. What is a night in the Casbah without a little of the exotic? Think about coming as a bellydancer, with baggy pants gathered at the ankle with elastic, and a tight midriff top. (Watch a rerun of *I Dream of Jeannie* to perfect this look.) A large faux gem in the belly button is a sexy accessory. Lots of dangling necklaces and long, hanging earrings add splash to the costume.

For a little "local color," you may choose to come as a "Blue Man of the Sahara." These nomads wear flowing deep-blue robes over their jellabas, blue twisted turbans, and are said even to have a blue tint to their skin. Achieving this very exotic look is fairly easy: Take an old white sheet, dye it indigo blue, then just drape it around you. Fashion a turban from a towel or a piece of the dyed sheet. Suggestion: For authenticity, don't shower the day of the party.

ACTIVITIES

Aboard Ship

On the boat (in reality the dining room), play poker for treasures, much as it was done in the movie *The Black Stallion*. (Rent the film before the party to get tips.) In fact, "treasures" can be dime-store trinkets and various odds and ends found around the house. Rhinestones become diamonds, a little metal horse is an Etruscan artifact, plastic beads are priceless heirlooms. Group consensus determines the relative value of each item.

In the Casbah

Bargaining—whether in the spice market, the camel market,

or the numerous souks deep within the medina—is very much a part of life in the Casbah. Therefore, ask your guests to come with a shopping bag, and instruct them to continue to barter with each other all evening long, using the treasures won on the ship.

Explain that certain "treasures" were marked earlier in the evening and that those who obtained the marked treasures will be awarded prizes.

A Performance of Harem Dancers

Prearrange for three or four of your more outgoing female guests to give a performance. They can choose their music from some of the marvelous selections that follow. (Make sure that you have prizes for these daring dancers.)

MUSIC

You will be surprised at the number of CDs and tapes available in the "International/Arabic-Muslim" section of a large record store. If these tapes are not readily available where you live, contact the record company directly.

Here are some choices:

- *Claude Ciari Plays the Hits of Fairuz and Mohamed Abdel Wahab* (All further description on this tape was in Arabic, but the case featured a most alluring photo of a woman wear-

February 28—M*A*S*H Final Episode

Celebrate the most widely watched show in television history with a Remember M*A*S*H Party. The final M*A*S*H episode was shown on this date in 1983 and captured 77 percent of the viewing public, making it one of the most watched shows in television history.

ing a very brief bikini, on her hands and knees on the beach.)
- *Gnawa Music of Marrakesh, Night Spirit Masters.* According to a quote from Robert Palmer of *Rolling Stone,* this tape offers "powerful, often spooky performances in the heart of the ancient medina. . . ." (Axiom, distributed by Island Records, 825 Eighth Avenue, NY, NY 10019.)
- *The Master Musicians of Jajouka,* featuring Bachir Attar (Axiom, distributed by Island Records, 825 Eighth Avenue, NY, NY 10019.)

Believe it or not, I actually found a collection of "belly dance" music in the Arabic music section of a larger record store. CDs available include:

Belly Dance Volume 3 (Voice of Lebanon, produced by Robert Khayat & Co.)

Best of Belly Dance from Egypt and Lebanon (ARC Music)

Picture Yourself Belly Dancing (Monitor International)

Another excellent idea is to browse through a good used-record store. I found one classic oldie: *Port Said: The Music of the Middle East,* featuring Mohammed El-Bakkar and his Oriental Ensemble (Audio Fidelity).

For more of a 1920s fox-trot approach to Middle Eastern music, think about two albums produced by the contemporary New Leviathan Oriental Fox Trot Orchestra: *S.S. Leviathan* or *Old King Tut,* which includes a cut, "If You Sheik on Your Mama, Your Mama's Gonna Sheba on You." (What a pity that this piece, written by Chris Smith in 1924, has no words.)

MARCH

March 10—First Paper Money Issued in the United States

Depending on the state of the economy, you may want to use this date as an excuse for an Inflation Party or a Celebrate Capitalism Party. Monopoly money, money toilet paper in the bathroom, and a giant dollar bill as a backdrop are suggested props.

PRIZES

Gifts for the harem dancers could be tacky, dangling costume jewelry. Custom-made "Casbah" T-shirts should prove a big hit. Depending on your party budget and number of guests, you may want to think about having custom T-shirts made for everyone attending. (See page 139.) A possible slogan for the shirts could be: I'VE SURVIVED THE CASBAH or I'VE BEEN TO THE CASBAH (front) with AND BACK or AND SURVIVED (back).

March 14—Albert Einstein's Birthday

An excellent excuse for an $E = MC^2$ (Energy) Party or the Nerd Party. You can order a life-size cardboard likeness of Albert Einstein (see pages 134–35) to greet guests. Prize ideas from the Nerd Party could be used.

Go Fish

For our Casbah Party, I traveled on the ship as a Hassidic gem merchant, wearing black pants, a black vest (yes, recycled from my Western costume), a broad-brimmed black hat, a fake beard, and a tallis (prayer shawl), which was really my grandmother's old piano shawl. As the evening wore on, the betting got heavier. At one point, the Texas millionaire made a substantial raise—a plastic airplane (representing a Learjet). Everyone else folded, not wanting to get involved in such high stakes. After a long, tense look at my cards, I said, "To match this bet I'll need some real gold," then reached into my sack and came up with a plastic bag filled with water—and two live goldfish—purchased that afternoon at Woolworth's. Needless to say, I won the hand.

Note: If you do this, make sure that the fish are in a large plastic bag with lots of water and air. A one-quart plastic container would also work, and could be left uncovered until just before the game.

Anything for a Dirham!

One reason we decided to throw a Casbah Party was because we had been to Morocco and, except for one unfortunate incident when we were chased by bandits in the Rif Mountains, were totally mesmerized by the sights and sounds of the country. Especially intriguing were the medinas of Fez and Marrakesh.

One memorable evening we returned to Djemaa-el-Fna square, at the entrance to the medina in Marrakesh. There, water sellers with ornate brass water containers on their backs circle the square, snake charmers coax menacing cobras out of their baskets, and storytellers perform animated tales of the Arabian Nights. All very interesting—and colorful—but what fascinated us most was a truly unique act: a man with a trained donkey that would lie on the ground, cross its legs, and smoke a cigarette. Anything for a dirham!

Backdrop for A Night in the Casbah Party.
See instructions on page 132.

THE SPEAKEASY

It was a wild time. The days of F. Scott Fitzgerald and Zelda, the Valentine's Day Massacre, and, of course, flappers. It was a time of uninhibited dancing, when corruption was rampant, and (with the exception of Carry Nation and an avid band of prohibitionists) booze flowed freely—just not in public.

Speakeasies sprang up across the country, especially in big cities, where the illegal "hooch" and "sauce" was consumed by the gallon nightly. By 1925 some 100,000 speakeasies dotted Manhattan alone. Corrupt cops were on the take, and mobsters made millions.

It was an intriguing time that would be really fun to re-create at a Speakeasy Party.

INVITATIONS

Make your friends feel special by mailing them a personal membership card for The Speakeasy. Invitations should note that there is no entrance fee, but requirements include period dress and a willingness to Charleston.

The card should give the date, time, and the all-important secret code word. Make it clear that in order to gain admittance to the party, the card must be shown at the door. And if guests forget the code word, then they may as well forget coming!

Here's a sample:

```
┌─────────────────────────────────────┐
│  JOE'S JOINT                         │
│       It will be the cat's pajamas!  │
│                                      │
│   Date:                              │
│                                      │
│   Time:                              │
│                                      │
│   Address:                           │
│                                      │
│   Secret Code Word:  TESSIE          │
│   R.S.V.P.:                          │
│            membership card           │
└─────────────────────────────────────┘
```

Helpful hint: Omit descendants of the Women's Christian Temperance Union, the Anti-Saloon League of America, or the National Prohibition Party from your invitation list. Party poopers to be sure!

You also might think about enclosing a brief instructional manual on how to Charleston.

DECOR

Remember that speakeasies were illegal and that your guests won't be pleased if the party is raided and they're carted off to spend the night in the slammer, so be careful to be authentic and have a good "bouncer" at the front door. If your house already has a peephole in the door, make sure you use it. If not, make a fake door with one. And don't stop there. Federal agents and greedy cops were a dime a dozen during Prohibition, so make sure to give the guests a good "once-over" with a wary eye. After they show their cards, open the door a crack and make a closer inspection. No federal agents here, thank you.

Have lots of potted (no pun intended) palms (real or fake) around the room, as well as any art deco-style accessories.

You also may want to create a feeling for the era by having fake newspapers around, with headlines such as "Babe Ruth Hits 60 Home Runs for Yankees," "Charles Lindbergh Solos the Atlantic in Spirit of St. Louis," or "Admiral Byrd Reaches the Antarctic."

The liquor table should have the booze properly labeled: hooch, bathtub gin, red ink (homemade wine), Virginia Dare (22 percent "medicinal" tonic sure to put hair on your chest), sauce, and moonshine.

Have a reprint of section 1 of the XVIII Amendment to the Constitution:

> **After one year from ratification of this article the manufacture, sale, or transportation of intoxicating liquors within, the importation thereof into, or the exportation thereof from the United States and all territory subject to the jurisdiction thereof for beverage purposes is hereby prohibited.**

You may wish to make this into a dartboard.

March 23—Near-Miss Day

In 1989 a mountain-size asteroid passed within 500,000 miles of earth. An excellent way to celebrate this near miss is a Thank Your Lucky Stars Party. Celestial decor and costumes would be appropriate.

COSTUMES

Just imagine you are going back in time to the Roaring '20s. Women have just experienced a newfound freedom: along with bobbing their hair, they have shed their corsets, and taken up smoking and exposing their legs.

Here's a chance to see how you'd do as a flapper. Survey the vintage clothing shops for some of the wonderful beaded dresses with uneven hemlines, or if you want to take the economical route, take a stab at making your own. (See pages 30–31.) Shoes should be high heels with either T or ankle straps. Spit curls and beauty marks would certainly be appropriate, as would a long cigarette holder or a sequined headband with a plume. And in this era, stockings rolled below the knees were not the sign of a bag lady. No way. Flappers were just advertising that there was nothing under that dress to hold them up! Other accessories to consider would be a steel-beaded handbag and lots of long beads and large jewelry. Any Egyptian-style accessory would be very "in."

Makeup should be exaggerated (though not Tammy Faye exaggerated!). Wear scarlet lipstick and go for dramatic eyes. Furs (recycled from the Politically Incorrect Party) are always chic.

Men should consider black dinner jackets and bow ties. An ascot, white silk scarf, or top hat would be a great accessory. If you choose to be more informal, wear a double-breasted suit and a fedora. Slicked-back hair parted in the middle would certainly be fashionable.

And don't forget that secret supply of hooch, carried in either a hip flask or hot water bottle.

Another idea would be to come as a specific character from the era. If glamour is your thing, think about coming as F. Scott or Zelda Fitzgerald, Clara Bow, Rudolph Valentino, or Rudy Vallee. If sports is your milieu, consider Jack Dempsey, Gene Tunney, or Babe Ruth.

If you are inclined to mix things up a little, consider coming as one of the bootleggers, such as Al Capone, his partner Johnny

Torrio, or Bugs Moran (but remember that it was Bugs's boys who fell victim to Capone in the famous St. Valentine's Day Massacre).

Or shake things up a bit by coming as an undercover federal agent. Re-create Eliot Ness or, better yet, Izzy Einstein (with or without his trusty sidekick, Moe Smith). "Who's Izzy?" you ask. Said to be so good at disguises that he could make a chameleon blush for lack of variations, Izzy was a federal agent known to masquerade as a member of the orchestra (he could blow a mean trombone), a truck driver, or even a pickle salesman. He is credited with some 40,000 speakeasy raids in New York. For this part, wear padding and a boater, and chew on a big stogie. In his own words, "Who'd ever think a fat man with pickles was an agent?"

JIVE TALK

Like any other party, you can't just dress the part, you also have to speak it. So practice up on your speakeasy vocabulary:

> Copacetic—excellent
> Flat tire—bore
> Giggle water—liquor
> Gin mill—speakeasy
> Hooch—liquor
> It's the bunk—disbelief
> Jazzbo, cakeater, or jellybean—boyfriend
> Nifty or the nuts—cool
> Ossified—drunk
> The real McCoy—the real thing
> Snugglepup—a heavy necker

So when you enter, exclaim "Hot diggity, this is the cat's pajamas!"

MUSIC

The correct Flapper-era music is key to this party. Find a recording of The Charleston. Other top hits from the era include:

> "Ain't She Sweet (Just a-Walkin' Down the Street)"
> "Ain't We Got Fun"
> "I'm Just Wild About Harry"
> "I'm Looking Over a Four-Leaf Clover"
> "'Way Down Yonder in New Orleans"

ACTIVITIES

The Charleston is a must, so make sure that everyone has the chance to learn. Encourage people to practice before they arrive, but also offer a quick tutorial (à la Arthur Murray) once guests arrive. While it would be helpful to know the correct steps, remember that by 1925, there were at least 400 different variations—all "undignified"—so what the heck, let people make it up as they go along. Don't worry if your guests take off in an entirely unorthodox and original direction. Isadora Duncan isn't going to turn over in her grave.

The Basic Charleston

Believe it or not, I found a "how to" dance instructional record for The Charleston at our local library: *Betty White's How to Charleston* (1960 Conversa-phone Institute, Inc. "Successful Teaching Methods Since 1911"). This record, complete with an instructional manual, teaches you the basics of the forward and back kick, the single diagonal kick, the more challenging Charleston Twist (which involves pivoting in and out on the balls of your feet), and the out-of-control double kick. If you aren't lucky enough to find Betty White's instructional record, just give your guests these simple guidelines:

- The basic step is a toes-in heels-out twisting step, performed solo, with a partner, or in a group.
- The knees are bent, then straightened as your feet pivot in and out, with your free leg kicking out.
- The key is to isolate body parts, swinging hips, shoulders, arms, legs—and anything else that seems appropriate—as you pitch your body weight forward. If women wear long beads, use one hand to swing these in time to the music.

My recommendation would be to rent the video of *The Great Gatsby* to pick up what you can and make up the rest as you go along. A lot of zest and enthusiasm can go a long way—especially if the hooch is flowing freely.

If the crowd is up to it, have a Charleston contest, or make a Charleston conga line.

Pin the Bottle on Carry Nation

She had a sad life: a crazy mother and an alcoholic husband, but lighten up, Carry! Hey, we've all got our burdens. Old Carry was certainly no friend of those who wanted to take life in the fast lane and certainly no hero at the speakeasies. So get out your frustration with Carry's rigid ways and play Pin the Bottle on Carry Nation, a version of Pin the Tail on the Donkey.

APRIL

April 12—First Man in Space

On this day in 1961, Yuri Gagarin spent 108 minutes orbiting the earth. This would be an excellent day to host a Space Cadets Party. Costume possibilities are limitless, as the theme could be taken quite literally or in its broader context. This day (or July 20, 1969, the date of the moon landing) would also be a great time to invite some friends over for a screening of *Amazon Women on the Moon*, an underrecognized, but very funny, offbeat film. Other movie choices could include *Destination Moon*, *First Men in the Moon*, or *Plan 9 from Outer Space*, labeled the most popular of the so-bad-it's-good movies by one video guide.

Look up a biography of Carry, photocopy her picture, and blow it up. Then make a fifth of gin out of cardboard. Take turns "pinning the bottle on Carry." The one who gets the bottle in the most humorous place wins.

PRIZES

What could be a more appropriate prize than liquor? Go to the local package store and buy those mini, nip-size bottles of assorted liquors. Then paste on your own "Speakeasy" labels. (Blank labels can be purchased at an office supply store. They can be printed either on a computer or by hand.)

April 13—Samuel Beckett's Birthday

Celebrate the Irish playwright's birth (1906) with an Absurd Party. For ideas, borrow a copy of *Endgame* or *Waiting for Godot* from the library.

Surprise Your Friends (and Yourself) by Making Your Own Flapper Dress

Okay, so you're not a seamstress. Neither am I. But you don't have to be a successful dressmaker to master this easy task. In fact, while it would be extremely helpful to have a sewing machine, you could get by without one.

Here's how: First, take the following measurements: your width around your widest part (probably your bust or your buns); your length from under your arms to about three inches above your knee. You'll come up with something like thirty-eight-inch width by twenty-nine-inch length. Add a few inches to each to allow for hems and seams, so you'll be looking for a piece of material that is about forty-five inches wide by thirty-six inches long. Then, for the shoulder straps, measure the distance over your shoulders from the under your arms in front, to the same position on your back (approximately eighteen inches).

Now comes the fun part: Take a field trip to your local fabric store and pick out some very showy material. (I fell in love with magenta satin.) Material comes in bolts that are either thirty-six or forty-five inches wide, so you'll probably only need to buy about one yard of cloth. Don't be skimpy. It's far better to have too much than too little. Nobody wants to be in a strait-jacket dress for an evening of dancing!

While at the fabric store, also buy some sequined trim (about one to two inches wide) for shoulder straps, and enough fringe (at least three inches long) to go around the top and bottom of the dress. (To be safe, buy two and a half to three yards.) Because I did a quick and dirty sewing job, I also bought enough Velcro for the length of the dress so I didn't have to fuss with putting in a zipper. And don't forget to buy matching thread.

Now for the nitty-gritty of sewing. The simplest method is to wrap the material around you, sew hems around the top and bottom, and sew in the Velcro on the side, so you can get in and out of the dress. Then sew on the shoulder straps and the fringe. If you are a little more ambitious and want a more fitted dress, cut the material in two, and make side seams. This way, you can add darts for your bust before you sew the side seams together. Voilà! You have a flapper dress.

To accessorize, buy enough sequined elastic trim (about two inches wide) to go around your head. Safety-pin it closed, and add a feather for effect.

Who Said I Wouldn't Wear a G-String?

One year, as a joke (I hope) a friend gave me a turquoise sequined G-string and matching pasties. To know my '60s feminist orientation is to know how absurd this gift was.

But much to my friend's surprise, I actually wore the G-string to our Speakeasy Party. The only catch was that I wore it on my head, as a rather elaborate and eye-catching headband. All I did was buy a sequined decal, which I safety-pinned to the G-string, and added feathers (from a feather duster that I bought at Woolworth's).

The pasties—which could have made lovely matching earrings—stayed at home in my drawer.

Backdrop for The Speakeasy Party.
See instructions on page 132.

The Politically Incorrect Party

In recent years, we have become more and more aware of "politically correct" (PC) behavior. Recycling is PC, smoking is politically incorrect (PIC). Using the term "Native American" is PC; teaching your children to play cowboys and Indians is PIC. One could go on and on: Reading Joan Didion is PC; reading Jacqueline Susann is PIC. (Though if you must, the least you can do is disguise the book with a homemade bookcover made out of a brown paper grocery bag—an act that is, in itself, PC.) Get it?

So if you are tired of getting dirty looks from the person behind you in line at the grocery store when you accept a plastic bag (and feel forced to say that you will certainly recycle it), or if you still buy maraschino cherries or veal, perhaps you would like to force all your friends to be politically incorrect for an evening.

PARTY PLANNING

For this party, it may be fun to have a preparty planner, where you invite a small group of friends over for a brainstorming session. Order out for pizza (still PC, I think), and make lists of everything you can think of that is politically incorrect: books, movies, songs, food, people, and the like. Then incorporate them into the party.

INVITATIONS

This is the time to use your rubber-stamp catalogs (see pages 129–30). Order one of the ecology stamps (the earth, a leopard, or an elephant, for example), and then either stamp or draw the international sign for "no"—a red circle with a diagonal line through it—over the stamp. Here's a sample:

On the back, write: "A whole forest was destroyed to make this card."

When mailing to couples, make sure that the invitations are addressed to the husband "and the little woman," or, at the least, to Mr. and Mrs. John Doe, especially if the woman has kept her own name.

SETTING THE MOOD

Make sure that all your plates and utensils are plastic and disposable. No recycling here! Cups should be Styrofoam.

In setting up the food table, make signs such as:

For tuna:
OOPS, CAUGHT-A-FEW-DOLPHINS-BY-ACCIDENT TUNA SALAD

For chicken:
CHICKENS IN THIS DISH SUFFERED IN SMALL, CROWDED CAGES

For shrimp:
DENUDED MANGROVE FORESTS OFF THE COASTS OF TROPICAL
NATIONS TO BRING YOU THIS DISH

For red meat:
RAIN FORESTS IN SOUTH AND CENTRAL AMERICA WERE CLEARED TO
RAISE THE CATTLE YOU ARE NOW EATING

In front of the green salad, have a sign reading:
PICKED BY NON-UNION WORKERS

Also, on your tablecloth, have a sign that reads:
MADE IN A FOREIGN SWEATSHOP BY EXPLOITED CHILDREN

On the door to the kitchen, have a sign saying:
GALS ONLY

Ask men to make sure that they leave the seat up after visiting the toilet.

April 15—Income Tax Day

Drown your IRS sorrows with friends. Suggestion: If some friends are lucky enough to be getting refunds, ask them to bring the beer.

**Backdrop for The Politically Incorrect Party.
See instructions on page 132.**

COSTUMES

It goes without saying that any fur—and especially the fur of an endangered species (fake, of course)—would make an excellent costume. You could put a sign on your fur: IT'S NOT FAKE ANYTHING, IT'S A REAL ENDANGERED SPECIES!

Any leopard-skin outfit would be wonderful, as would faux crocodile shoes, belts, or handbags. Any jewelry that could pass for ivory would make an excellent accessory.

Helpful hint: Fake fur in a variety of species is available at your local fabric store for approximately $13.00 per yard. Our store also had leopard-print stretch fabrics.

You could think about carrying a vial that contains an imitation aphrodisiac made from a rhino's horn.

Couples could think about making a politically incorrect statement by coordinating their outfits. Here are some examples:

- Have the man come as a white-collar worker and the woman as a secretary (carrying a steno pad and coffee).
- The man can dress as a doctor and the woman as the nurse.
- Have the man come as a sleazy pornography producer and the women as a sex kitten.

Other costume ideas include: an American Indian (for this party "Native American" won't do), carrying a tomahawk and a scalp; a representative from a chemical company, carrying pesticides (Agent Orange, DDT, etc.); a great white hunter; a real estate developer who is trying to build condominiums on Walden Pond; or a taxidermist, specializing in endangered species.

You also may want to come as a particular person, such as Frank Purdue, Donald Trump, Howard Stern, Imelda Marcos, Hitler, Mussolini, Saddam Hussein, James Watt, or one of the Gabor sisters, Zsa Zsa or Eva.

DECORATING

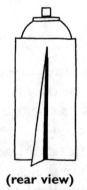

(rear view)

Make a giant aerosol spray can (see instructions),* and drape the doors and windows with plastic wrap. Make sure you put out lots of big ashtrays.

---

*Instructions for Two-Dimensional Cutout of Aerosol Spray Can:
Buy a sheet of foam core (largest size, 4 feet by 8 feet, is best, but it may be too difficult to transport) at a large art supply store. (Call first to check on availability.) Sketch the image of the can on the sheet, and using a matte knife or hand-held electric saw,

Make giant posters:

WANTED: WOMEN WHO WILL SHOW A LOT OF LEG AND WORK FOR LESS

HOMOPHOBES FOR A BETTER AMERICA

NEVER MET AN ENDANGERED SPECIES I DIDN'T LIKE—TO EAT, THAT IS!

Some plastic grass or any room decoration that could resemble scrimshaw or ivory would add a nice touch.

ACTIVITIES

For this party, role-playing for the entire evening is essential. Men should make sexist remarks and women should play the role of dumb blondes. When a well-endowed woman passes by, the man could comment on the nice set of "jungle drums."

First, when guests arrive, hand out a list of politically incorrect films, books, and music for your guests to refer to in conversation during the evening.

Create a Politically Incorrect Quiz.

Consider playing Politically Incorrect Charades. Divide your guests (yourself included) into two teams. Each team should be given fifteen minutes to come up with some good politically incorrect titles, which are then put into a hat for the other team to act out. Alternatively, you may want to make the competition more difficult by taking "normal" songs, movies, or books, and turning them into politically incorrect titles. Just to get you going, here are a few suggestions:

---

cut out the image. Using another piece of foam core, cut out a triangle (see illustration) for support—like a giant picture frame or cut-out figure. Color the can using markers or paint. Note: for those on a tight budget, scavenge around for a large appliance box and use that instead of the foam core.

Song Titles

"Crocodile Rock"
"Ebony and Ivory"
"Singing in the [Acid] Rain"

You may opt for something a little easier. Consider buying *Mad Libs*, a party game where one person asks the rest of the party to fill in missing nouns, verbs, and adjectives to make a humorous story. Instead of using just any word, use only politically incorrect ones.

A sure crowd-pleaser would be the *very* x-rated Pin the Macho on the Man or Pin the Boobs on the Babe game (put out by Pipedream Produces, Van Nuys, CA). The Macho version includes a 24-by-36-inch color poster of the Macho Man, fifteen cartoon anatomical "units" for pinning, and ten generic "units" for the more creative participants. Imagine what the Babe version includes!

A potentially less offensive optional activity could be a talent show. Tell guests in advance that they should bring their own tapes for lip-synching (or for those who have more nerve, background music) for performing a politically incorrect song. Provide the guests with the following list of politically incorrect music to choose from.

MAY

First Saturday in May—Kentucky Derby Day

Have a cocktail party around the "Run for the Roses"—the first leg in the Triple Crown. If you're ambitious, you can set up a bookmaker's window and have your friends wager on the race. Suggest that guests come in Churchill Downs attire—for women, that would include the mandatory large-brimmed hats.

Music

"Bad Girls" by Donna Summer
"Calendar Girl" by Neil Sedaka
"Don't Go Near the Indians" by Rex Allen
"Follow the Boys" by Connie Francis
"The Girl Can't Help It" by Little Richard
"Girls Just Want to Have Fun" by Cyndi Lauper
"Girls Were Made to Love" by Eddie Hodges
"Half Breed" by Cher
"He Hit Me (And It Felt Like a Kiss)" by The Crystals
"100 Pounds of Clay" by Gene McDaniels
"If You Want to Be Happy (Make an Ugly Woman Your Wife)" by Jimmy Soul
"Indian Reservation" by The Raiders
"I Will Follow Him" by Little Peggy March
"Little Bitty Pretty One" by Thurston Harris
"Morning Train (Nine to Five)" by Sheena Easton
"My Ding-A-Ling" by Chuck Berry
"Party Doll" by Buddy Knox/The Rhythm Orchids
"Pretty Girls Everywhere" by Eugene Church
"Shop Around" by The Miracles
"Short Fat Fanny" by Larry Williams
"Short People" by Randy Newman—Yes, we know it's a spoof, but it gets listed anyway!
"Short Shorts" by Jerry Lee Lewis
"Stand by Your Man" by Tammy Wynette

May 11—Salvador Dali's Birthday

Celebrate this Spanish painter's birthday with a Surreal Party. A backdrop could be the famous dripping clock. Everyone— women as well as men—should honor Dali (who died in 1989 at the age of eighty-four) by wearing a long, pencil-thin mustache.

"That's What Girls Are Made For" by The Spinners
"Travelin' Man" by Ricky Nelson
"Watermelon Man" by Mongo Santamaria
"You Talk Too Much" by Joe Jones
"(You're) Havin' My Baby" by Paul Anka (with Odia Coates)

PRIZES

A copy of *Playboy, Hustler,* or *Penthouse* is always tacky—and politically incorrect.

Also consider any number of books, doodle books, games, or playing cards put out by Ivory Tower Publications, 125 Walnut Street, Watertown, MA 02172, (617) 924-9078. Sample titles include: *Working Girls Doodle Book, Working Man's Sex Fantasy Doodle Book,* and *A Hard Man Is Good to Find.* Politically incorrect boxed games include: Strip Poker, Potty Pot Shots, and Dirty Old Maid.

A great "self-help" prize is *The Official Politically Correct Dictionary and Handbook* by Henry Beard and Christopher Cerf (Villard, 1993).

Other prizes that cost very little can be found at any large toy store. In a recent trip to Toys 'R' Us, I found a Seven-Piece Combat Force Combat Set that included, among other things, a plastic Uzi, .45 automatic weapon, and two grenades; a Brave Set that included a tomahawk, knife, and headdress; and a whole host of politically incorrect Barbies, including Bay Watch Barbie, Bubble Angel Barbie, Butterfly Princess Barbie, and Tropical Splash Barbie.

A Sampling of Politically Incorrect Foods to Serve

Hors d'oeuvres

Cheese that comes out of an aerosol spray can
Canapés made with Wonder Bread

Desserts

Anything made with Cool Whip
Ding Dongs
Jell-O
Marshmallows
Twinkies

Drinks

Anything with Red Dye #2
Kool-Aid

FADED FADS

❋

Whether it was a Hula Hoop, a troll, or a Pet Rock, at one point or another, we've all succumbed to the totally pointless crazes that have swept the country. Let's face it: Fads are as American as motherhood and apple pie. So why not pay homage to them with a Faded Fads Party? Ask your friends over for a walk down memory lane and reconstruct some of the famous "hot" trends that have swept the country.

The most recent fads will, of course, come to mind first: roller blading, trolls (again!), neon clothing, friendship bracelets, Power Rangers, Teenage Mutant Ninja Turtles, Cabbage Patch Kids, Barney, and for the more daring (or crazy), tattoos and body piercing. But encourage your guests also to consider going back in time to come as goldfish swallowers, marathon dance contestants, or members of a panty raid (an idea that can cross over to the Politically Incorrect Party).

INVITATIONS

An easy way to get into the fads theme early would be by sending a Rubik's Cube invitation. Just trim a piece of $8^1/_2$-by-11-inch paper so that it will fold into a square. Then divide the cover into nine squares (like a tic-tac-toe board), and randomly color the squares with six colors: white, blue, yellow, green, red, and orange. If you don't want to bother with color, make the grid and leave all the squares white. Then label it "Idiot's Rubik's Cube."

Inside you can lightly repeat the grid, and write all the key information—date, time, location, and fad dress required—in the boxes.

DECOR

You can have a lot of fun with this one. If you are feeling extravagant, spring for a lava lamp or two. And think about black lights and Day-Glo. You just can't have too many happy faces on the walls. You also might want to re-create enlarged buttons from the '60s or '70s. Some classics are: DON'T TAKE DRUGS, GIVE THEM TO ME; LEGALIZE BROWN RICE; AMERICA HAS GONE TO POT; GO NAKED; SAVE WATER, SHOWER WITH A FRIEND; and the classic, TUNE IN, TURN ON, DROP OUT.

You also may want to make a big sign KILROY WAS HERE.

May 12—National Limerick Day

Observe the birthday of English artist and author Edward Lear (1812–1888) with a Limerick Party. Guests could be asked to bring a limerick with them, or once the party is under way, you could spontaneously make up your own, going around the room and having each person add a line. "There once was a woman named Nancy. Young boys were always her fancy. . . ." No minors, please. Need ideas? Consult *World's Best Limericks*, compiled by Nick Beilson (Peter Pauper Press, 1994) or *The Lure of the Limerick* by William S. Baring-Gould (Clarkson N. Potter, Inc., 1963).

COSTUMES

One option is to resurrect some of the more tacky or outrageous clothing fads from the last few decades, such as Nehru jackets (worn with a turtleneck and peace medallion, of course), Earth Shoes, micro-miniskirts, bell bottoms, hot pants, tie-dyed shirts, go-go boots, or polyester leisure suits. In fact, there is no rule against mixing and matching. How about a nice pair of hot pants with a Nehru jacket? A mood ring could make a great accessory with any outfit.

Don't forget the fabulous '50s. A nice poodle skirt would be a sure crowd pleaser. If you can't find one in a vintage clothing store, think about making your own from felt, using permanent marker to draw on the poodle, and then gluing on rhinestones for the poodle's eyes and collar.

A second option would be to dress as one of the fads, such as Chiquita Banana, Batman, a Smurf, Pac-man, Bart Simpson, a Slinky, a Couch Potato, Barbie (with or without Ken), a yo-yo, Gumby, Howdy Doody, a Rubik's Cube, or the first great baby boomer hero, Davy Crockett.

And don't forget the *Star Wars* fad and the great cast of characters that it brought: Darth Vader, Princess Laya, R2D2, C-3PO, and the large, furry, and lovable Chewbacca.

Make sure that your language matches the fad period. Skateboarders should refer to everything as "bitchin'," tie-dye wearers should be "groovin' out" and "outtasight," and marathon dance couples should comment that everything is the "cat's pajamas."

May 17—New York Stock Exchange Established

In 1792 some two dozen merchants and brokers got together and established the "market." In good weather it was held under a tree on Wall Street; in bad weather it moved to a coffeehouse. Come dressed as your favorite white-collar criminal, or just drape yourself in *The Wall Street Journal.* Use your imagination for this one—but no live bulls, please!

If you don't have time to put a costume together—and you're a little on the daring side—consider taking the easy way out and coming as a streaker. It may be smart to wear a trench coat, at least while en route to the party. Think about purchasing a pair of novelty underwear (or for women, a bikini), but don't let on that there is anything underneath. Let the crowd wonder: Are you or aren't you?

FOOD

We are just as fad oriented in food as we are in clothing and toys. Why not set out a fondue pot, baked Brie, pigs in a blanket, sushi, tofu, banana bread, and, of course, an assortment of quiches?

Check out the local Toys 'R' Us for the latest fad candy. I found Power Ranger candy dispensers, Gummy Rangers, and mini-troll graham snacks. Also consider the old standards: Cracker Jacks, Tootsie Rolls, and Pez.

Make sure to have a number of sand candles on hand.

Get paper plates, napkins, and cups of the latest fads. You can almost always find Mickey Mouse. Past and present favorites also include Barney, Teenage Mutant Ninja Turtles, Batman, Aladdin, the Lion King, and X-Men.

ACTIVITIES

This is primarily a dancing party—with a twist. Literally. Make tapes that include all the fad dances for the last thirty years, including:

the Bunny Hop
disco (à la *Saturday Night Fever*)
the Freddie
the Frug
the Hully-Gully

the Jerk
the Mashed Potato
the Monkey
the Pony
the Shimmy
the Skate
the Stroll
the Swim
the Twist
the Watusi

Don't be afraid to throw in a few nondancing "fad" songs, like Alvin and the Chipmunks singing "The Chipmunk Song," Allan Sherman's "Hello Mudduh, Hello Fadduh," "Purple People Eater," "Witch Doctor," or "The Monster Mash."

THE FAD DANCE RECALL CONTEST

Before the party, make a special tape that includes about one minute of at least eight of the fad dances. Then once the crowd is up and dancing, ask for three or four volunteers. Explain that you've made the tape and that they will be asked to identify and perform the dance as soon as it comes on the tape. The crowd will judge the best performance. (Just for fun, at the end of the tape, add some breakdance music and see how quickly your contestants can adapt.)

Of course, all contestants should receive prizes.

HULA HOOP CONTEST

If your party is outdoors, you are sure to have a great time with a Hula Hoop contest. You'll be surprised to see that the hoop that, in 1958, you twirled for hours now falls quickly to your ankles in a matter of seconds.

LIMBO CONTEST

If the party is indoors and you don't own a mansion, substitute a limbo contest for the Hula Hoop contest.

Taken from a sacred West Indian funeral rite, the limbo craze hit big in the early 1960s. Given exposure in the 1960 film *Where the Boys Are*, this dance had otherwise sane suburbanites performing weird body contortions in an attempt to dance under a pole.

Don't fret if you can't find one of the original Wham-O Limbo Party Games. Make do by asking any two guests suffering from back problems (or just two guests who don't want to risk orthopedic injury and gross humiliation) to serve as the pole holders. Put on a recording of Chubby Checker's "Limbo Rock," form a line, and voilà—you're limboing! Once any part of your body touches the pole (yes, well-endowed women are at a distinct disadvantage here), you're eliminated. After each successful round, the pole is lowered a few inches. Keep going until you have one winner.

Try to find Chubby Checker's *Limbo Party* album, containing such classics as "Mary Ann Limbo," "Lala Limbo," and "When the Saints Go Limbo In," or the less well-known follow-up album, *Let's Limbo More*.

The winner gets a real prize; the first person eliminated gets a workout book and tube of Ben-Gay.

May 22—Sir Arthur Conan Doyle's Birthday

Pay homage to one of the world's most famous and eccentric detectives, Mr. Sherlock Holmes, on this day. You could have a Sherlock Holmes Party, setting up your home as his rooms at 221B Baker Street, or think of another creative mystery party.

FUN AND GAMES FOR
THE NON-MOVERS AND SHAKERS

For your more sedate guests, have a Ouija board and a set of Tarot cards available for fortune-telling.

PRIZES

America's biggest fad still makes a great prize. Believe it or not, Hula Hoops are still available at local toy stores. You might consider buying one for each guest. If you are having trouble finding them, contact Maui Toys, the manufacturer of Maui hoops (they look just like the real thing) from, would you believe, Youngstown, Ohio, (216) 747-4333.

Other suggested prizes include a Rubik's Cube; plastic Cali-

Backdrop for Faded Fads Party.
See instructions on page 132.

fornia Raisin figures; crystals; Silly Putty; Slinkies; stickers; troll dolls; Pez dispensers; Duncan Imperial yo-yos; or Mighty Morphin Power Ranger turbo-charged spinner tops, collectible magnets, bubble blasters, or sneaker toppers.

Some great variations of trolls are available. The Battle Trolls, for example, are Rambo-style critters, marketed as "big-haired dudes with bad attitudes." There are also Nasty Trolls ("Squeeze my tummy, I stick out my tongue and become a nasty troll"), Teenage Mutant Ninja Turtle Trolls, Treasure Trolls ("the friendly troll with a belly button wishstone), and last, but certainly not least, a Troll Barbie.

May 22—The Last Johnny Carson Show

Celebrate the end of an era with a party to honor the king of late-night television. Your guests can come as famous guests from the Carson-era *Tonight Show* (for example, Tiny Tim and Miss Vicki, who were married on the show) or as famous Carson characters, such as Carnac.

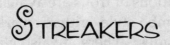STREAKERS

When jogging became a craze in the 1970s, some took it one step further, running naked. Initially streaking was confined primarily to college campuses, but by the time the fad peaked in 1974, streakers had made appearances at the Academy Award ceremonies, the Eiffel Tower in Paris, and St. Peter's Square in Rome.

Some notable streaking trivia:

Longest Streak:

Five hours, by Texas Tech students

Largest Streaks:

1,543 participants at the University of Georgia

Most Creative Streaks:

Harvard students streaking through an anatomy class wearing nothing but surgical masks.

A University of South Carolina streaker who ran into the library requesting a copy of *The Naked Ape.*

Most Political Streak:

The streaker who ran through the Hawaiian state legislature chamber, claiming to be "Streaker of the House."

Best Quote:

An Atlanta, Georgia, bus driver, who, when asked to identify the sex of streakers who ran through his bus, told police, "I couldn't tell. They were wearing masks."

GREAT ENTERTAINERS

For this party, all guests must come as a famous entertainer of their choice. The only catch—and it's a major one—is that when the "talent" portion of the evening is announced, guests will be asked to perform as their character.

The night we threw the Great Entertainers Party, we got a truly eclectic group of performers. Guests included: Janis Joplin, Alberta Hunter, Ethel Merman, Bob Marley, Maurice Chevalier and Hermione Gingold (from *Gigi*), Tina Turner, Stevie Wonder (whose braids were attached to a plastic headband), and Martha Reeves and the Vandellas.

May 24—Bob Dylan's Birthday

What better excuse for a '60s party? The answer is Blowin' in the Wind. Guests could be asked to bring their favorite '60s-era tape or LP—for authenticity, no CDs, please.

Other suggested entertainers could be: Gypsy Rose Lee (sure to get some attention if costuming is done correctly and gradually disappears as the evening wears on), Pee-wee Herman (either in character or wearing a trench coat), Mick Jagger (a pair of large wax lips would be a must), Marilyn Monroe, Sid Vicious, Joan Rivers (who just has to spend the evening asking all other guests "Can we talk?"), and Tiny Tim (with or without Miss Vicki).

Helpful Hint: Since performing is such an important part of this party, it's better to come as a singer or comic than a dramatic actor. Lip synching is far easier—and more of a crowd pleaser—than presenting a scene.

Guests must stay in character from the moment they enter the party. For example, Janis Joplin must constantly pop pills (in reality, sugar candies, in case any narcs are reading this), and Tina Turner must show a lot of leg.

One variation for this party would be to focus on musical entertainers from one era or decade. Take the '80s, for instance. Guests would have their choice of:

- Bruce Springsteen (shirt sleeves rolled up), for all those who want to be the ultimate blue-collar rock hero for a night.
- Madonna (lots of corset options here). You might want to have a copy of *Sex*, because as we all know, Madonna just can't get too much attention.
- Boy George (Culture Club). George O'Dowd certainly had his rough times, but for this party, leave his woes behind and enjoy the exaggerated rag-doll style clothes, the bizarre hats, and the outrageous makeup.
- Milli Vanilli. Long dreadlocks are the look here. And this entry will be a shoo-in to win the lip-synching contest!
- Also consider Cyndi Lauper, New Kids on the Block, Prince, MC Hammer, all the Ice men: Ice Cube, Ice T, and Vanilla Ice.

INVITATIONS

This is the perfect party to use your glitter and feathers. (See pages 128–30.) There is no such thing as "bad taste" or "too ostentatious" when it comes to the Great Entertainers Party. You can buy simple colored paper (neon would be good) and affix feathers and glitter.

An easier route would be to buy old postcards of classic entertainers. (Each can be different.)

Backdrop for the Great Entertainer Party.
See instructions on page 132.

DECOR

Here is a perfect time to use one or more of the life-size cutouts mentioned on pages 134–35. For example, Marilyn Monroe could meet guests at the door (or in an apartment building, as the guests get off the elevator), and Clint Eastwood, James Dean, or Betty Grable could be placed strategically around the room.

The backdrop can be a curtain, which must be hung in such a way that the performer can enter from behind for the performance.

Think about setting up a spotlight by using a powerful flashlight. We like to videotape the performances, but if your guests are new to this, it may inhibit them.

If you would like an outdoor motif, go Hollywood, using your palm trees and a reproduction of the famous Hollywood sign.

COSTUMES

A trip to a secondhand clothing store would be a great idea for this party. The more glitz and glitter, the better. Brightly colored boas and large pieces of costume jewelry make great accessories. If you're coming as a singer, check out record stores for photos on old albums or CDs. The library's popular culture section also may have books that will give you some good ideas.

For an evening gown, consider buying a few yards of some rich-looking satin or brocade, and then just draping it around you. (I've gone to more than one party in a floor-length gown held together only with safety pins.)

Furs, especially the kind that still have the heads on, are dynamite additions. (And can be recycled for the Politically Incorrect Party.)

JUNE

June I—Marilyn Monroe's Birthday

It is more than thirty years since this movie legend died on August 6, 1962, but the myth continues. Use this day to celebrate Marilyn's best movies or as an excuse for a Hollywood Party. One of the life-size cutouts of Marilyn (see page 135) is a must. Think about dressing up in glitzy '50s thrift shop clothes, or showing one of Marilyn's classic movies: *Gentlemen Prefer Blondes, How to Marry a Millionaire, Seven Year Itch, Bus Stop,* or my personal favorite, *Some Like It Hot.*

One rule of thumb for dressing will always hold true: the more ridiculous and exaggerated, the better. Your mother, like mine, may have taught you that understated is better, but clearly, she did not have a Great Entertainers Party in mind. Here "Gaudy is Great" should be your motto.

Helpful Hint from a guest: "Think twice about coming as a Rastafarian if you're bald." —Dr. Jerome J. Solomon

ACTIVITIES

This would be primarily a dancing party, but at some point during the evening, the celebrity look-alikes must be given the opportunity to do what they do best: perform.

Since your guests may be a little stage-shy, have them pick numbers out of a hat to determine the order of performances.

Each guest must bring a tape or CD with the appropriate music.

After the performances, have ballots ready, and cast your votes for the winning act and costume.

PRIZES

There are two prizes awarded: one for best costume and one for best act.

Get trophies inscribed at the local trophy store. Depending on

June 2—Marquis de Sade's Birthday

The Marquis de Sade—the inspiration for the word sadism—was born in Paris in 1740 and died in a lunatic asylum in 1814. The date of his birth presents a unique party opportunity for our kinkier partygoers: a time for those whips and chains to come out of the closet.

the crowd, you may wish to buy trophies that mimic the Grammies, or—if your crowd is like ours—it might be more appropriate to get a "horse's ass" or similar humorous trophies.

THE MICROPHONE: IT JUST FEELS RIGHT!

When you get up to perform, you've got to go with the flow. But it's hard to get into the swing of things without a mike in your hand. For our first performance party, we used a soap-on-a-rope microphone. But when one performer became overzealous, swinging the mike from hand to hand—and then dropping it—we ended up with soap chips. Great for the laundry, but hardly appropriate for the rest of the performers.

So our suggestion is to invest in a real but inexpensive mike. You can buy a new mike (intended for tape recorders) for about $12 and an amplifying mike beginning at about $18. Either looks great and has the right feel. Whether you actually plug it in is totally up to you—and your performers.

Anything for a Win?!?

One sure way to be a crowd pleaser—and possibly get extra votes—is by cross-dressing. Experience has shown that men dressed as women get a much better reaction than vice versa.

Not surprisingly, our highly competitive scientist—who will do just about anything for a win—has been one of our most frequent cross-dressers. So it wasn't surprising that his sister (who flew from Denver to Boston for this party) and I easily convinced him to join us as Martha Reeves and the Vandellas.

We got our costumes together pretty quickly. Only one obstacle remained: "intimate apparel" for our cross-dresser.

We headed for Filene's Basement. For those unfamiliar with the original Filene's Basement in downtown Boston, suffice to say that it's a place you can find some great bargains. It's also a place where you can find the weirdest, leftover clothing in the world.

We immediately headed for the "Automatically Reduced" table. In no time flat, we found a particularly dowdy cotton number, size 40 D, reduced to $2.50.

By this point, our "anything for a win" scientist was beginning to have second thoughts, and was standing by pretending that he had nothing to do with us. But before he realized it, we slipped it on over his sweater to test the fit. Just then a woman stopped her bargain hunting long enough to watch us. She looked over, smiled, and gave him a major thumbs-up sign, commenting "Lookin' good!"

Only he can say whether it was worth the humiliation. But that evening he fell off his high heels once, and we brought down the house with "Heat Wave."

THE NERD PARTY

One of our most successful parties was a fortieth-birthday Nerd Party. While I was lucky to have a true nerd (when I met Ken at an M.I.T. graduate student party, he was wearing his bell-bottom pants above his ankles—two years after bell bottoms were passé), this theme party would work well for someone who is borderline nerdy—or even for anyone who would just get a kick out of seeing all his or her friends parading around as geeks for an evening.

If you've had only limited exposure to real nerds, rent the video of *Revenge of the Nerds* or *Revenge of the Nerds II: Nerds in Paradise* for ideas.

INVITATIONS

It is important to establish the nerd theme from the outset. One way to do this is to create a really "geeky" invitation. We did this by sending out invitations in plastic pocket protectors (available at a stationery store), which were also stuffed with a plastic protractor.

If you want to go "digital," imitate a home page from the World Wide Web or send the invitations as if they are e-mail messages.

Whichever format you choose, make sure that the invitation emphasizes that all guests are to dress up as nerds. (You will be surprised to see how nerdy your friends can become from just one visit to the thrift shop!)

Since our nerd of honor went to M.I.T., we used an M.I.T. graphic on the cover (see sample), but you can just as easily use a picture of Hush Puppy shoes or a slide rule.

DECOR

Let your guests know where the nerd action is before they even enter the front door by buying a NERD CROSSING sign (18-inch square galvanized steel reproduction highway crossing sign) and putting it in front of your house the night of the party. This sign ($35) is available from the M.I.T. Museum Shop. (See page 140 for information on ordering.)

Once inside, have lots of old calculus books around as well as blue exam books. Calculators, protractors, compasses, graph pa-

---

June 6—National Yo-Yo Day

A perfect day for a Village Idiots Party. In addition to yo-yos, think about propeller beanies. Those who are diehard classical music fans can always bring a cello and come as Yo Yo Ma.

Come Help Ken

Celebrate

his $(6.3)^2$ Birthday

Date:

Time:

Place:

Bring $E=MC^2$ and

dancing shoes.

Nerd dress requested

RSVP:

per, and slide rules (if you can find them) are also nice additions. For our party—because we had a real nerd—we blew up old photos (yes, complete with white socks and a plaid jacket) to poster size.

Remember that nerds love science fiction, so make sure that you've got lots of sci-fi magazines or anthologies of *Analog* around. Specific books could include: *The Mathematical Tourist* by Ivars Peterson (W. H. Freeman, 1988), *Mathematical Carnival* by Martin Gardner (Vintage, 1965), and *QED: The Strange Theory of Light and Matter* by Richard P. Feynman (Princeton University Press, 1985).

Nerds love strategic games, so find some Avalon Hill games, such as Blitzkrieg, Waterloo, or Alexander the Great, and pray that the real nerds in the group don't start to play.

COSTUMES

This one is easy: polyester, polyester, and more polyester. Pants should be above the ankles, and you also should consider thin white short-sleeved dress shirts, pocket protectors, calculators attached to your belt, protective laboratory glasses, and taped-together eyeglasses (with an elastic headstrap). Footwear should be white crew socks with wing-tip shoes or sandals with socks. If you must wear a T-shirt, make sure that it is at least one size too small. It would be appropriate to have a math or debating club logo.

Think about buying two pairs of white crew socks with different colored stripes on top and wearing one of each. Hats with earflaps are a nice accessory. Women should consider hairnets and white Peter Pan–collared blouses with cardigan sweaters. Knee-

---

June 10—Prince Philip's Birthday

This would be an appropriate choice to honor anyone who tends to blend into the wood-work. Think about showing the 1933 movie *The Invisible Man*.

high stockings that stick out beneath a shapeless skirt would certainly be appropriate.

For our party, we placed a KICK ME sign on the back of our guest of honor. He wore it all evening.

Another option is to create your own "cyborg" outfit. For those who are unfamiliar with the term, a cyborg is a pioneer in human-machine interaction. "Wire" yourself with cables, antennas, and whatever else strikes your fancy. Remember that nothing is too weird or too outrageous.

ACTIVITIES

The main activity at our Nerd Party was dancing ('60s music, of course), but we had some "warm-up" activities to get the crowd going. These included the Nerd Quiz (see page 66) and a Pin the Slide Rule on the Nerd game.

PRIZES

A Nerd Party is not complete without a number of prizes for the guests. These are awarded throughout the evening for various contests. The first is given for the winner of the Nerd Quiz, which serves as an icebreaker early in the evening. The second is awarded for the winner of the Pin the Slide Rule on the Nerd contest. (You may consider a consolation prize for the person who places the slide rule in the most embarrassing part of the nerd's anatomy.)

June 17—Watergate Day

Celebrate the anniversary of the arrests at the Democratic National Headquarters in 1972. See the Watergate Party for details (pages 70–79).

PIN the on the NERD

**Backdrop for the Nerd Party.
See instructions on page 132.**

It is essential to make sure that the prizes are in keeping with the theme. To ensure this, a perfect place to shop is the M.I.T. Museum Shop—which has the finest and most creative selection of nerd gifts. For those of you not fortunate enough to live within

THE NERD QUIZ

Just because you dress like a nerd does not mean that you think like one. Here is a test to see if your guests have really gotten into their roles. After everyone has arrived, announce that, like all true nerds, they will be very pleased to be taking a surprise quiz. Explain that earlier in the day the guest of honor (the only true nerd in the group) was given ten questions to answer. The guests are now going to be asked to answer the same ten questions. Whoever matches the most answers with the real nerd wins.

(Note: Make sure that you have lots of Number 2 pencils for this activity.)

Here are some sample questions:

1. *What is the first thing a nerd does before making love?*

   a. sets his stopwatch

   b. puts on a Mitch Miller record for ambiance

   c. sets his VCR to tape *Star Trek*

2. *What is the first thing a nerd does after making love?*

    a. records lapsed time in the bedroom logbook
    b. puts on fresh jammies
    c. says, "Okay, now it's your turn"

3. *How many nerds does it take to replace a lightbulb?*

    a. none: lava lamps don't have lightbulbs
    b. one: provided the new bulb comes with instructions
    c. three: one to compute when the original lightbulb burned
        out, one to try to fix it, and one to install new solar panels

4. *What do nerds do on New Year's Eve?*

    a. try to pick up Eastern European folk songs on their shortwave radios
    b. unwrap their "This Day in Mathematics" calendars
    c. determine the number of people per square foot in Times Square

(Answers: b, a, c, c)

driving distance of Cambridge, Massachusetts, the Museum Shop fills mail orders. To get a catalog and place orders, contact

The M.I.T. Museum Shop
265 Massachusetts Avenue
Cambridge, MA 02139
617-253-4462
Fax: 617-253-8994
E-mail: mitshop@mit.edu

Here is a sampling of possible prizes that can be purchased:

- Fractal T-shirts—Simple mathematical formulae transformed into strikingly beautiful computer-generated images, for $16.95.
- *Math Magic* by Scott Flansburg (a.k.a. The Human Calculator, Harper Perennial, 1993) for $10.
- *Sex as a Heap of Malfunctioning Rubble: More of the Best of the Journal of Irreproducible Results*, edited by George H. Scherr (Workman, 1983), a bargain at $9.95.
- A copy of *The Journal of Irreproducible Results*, published bimonthly by Blackwell Scientific Publications, for $2.95.
- The Mathematical Calendar. Where else can you get a challenging new mathematical problem every day? $9.95.
- Professional-quality slide rules, from $9.95.
- A host of nerd T-shirts, including the ever-popular AND GOD SAID T-shirt. The front features the black hole with Schwarzschild radius, and the back Maxwell's equation. A NERD BEST-BUY at $12.95 each.
- Other smaller prizes include: the brain helmet ($2.95), a brain candle ($5.95), and a pair of 3-D wink specks ($1.95).

Norbert Wiener, the founding father of cybernetics, was certainly one of the most brilliant—and eccentric—M.I.T. professors. As one story goes, after he had stopped to chat with a colleague, he asked, "Which way was I going when I met you?" When the colleague told him, Wiener responded, "Then I must have had lunch."

THE WATERGATE PARTY

W ho knew what when? Re-create the political scandal of a generation with a party filled with intrigue and subplots. Bring out the old cast of characters: H. R. Haldeman, John Ehrlichman, John and Maureen Dean, John and Martha Mitchell, G. Gordon Liddy, and, of course, Richard Nixon.

This party can be done two ways: First, it could be held as a smaller mystery party, where every guest is told in advance which Watergate character he or she will be playing at the party. You'll have to do some research and, throughout the evening, try to vindicate your character. Feel free to produce your own "unauthorized" tapes to refute those handed over to the Justice Department.

JULY

The entire month of July is Anti-Boredom Month, sponsored by the Boring Institute. For more information, write to Alan Caruba, Box 40, Maplewood, NJ 07040.

Second, it could be a larger and looser party, where everyone just comes as the Watergate character of his or her choice. You'll probably end up with three or four Nixons, duplicate Martha Mitchells, and an assortment of "Deep Throats," but this will only add to the fun.

Take your pick. Either will make a great party!

To get in the proper mood, recommended reading includes *All the President's Men* by Carl Bernstein and Bob Woodward (Warner Books, 1975) (if you're not inclined to read the book, rent the movie); *Blind Ambition* by John Dean (Simon & Schuster, 1976); *The King and Us,* editorial cartoons by Conrad (Clymer); or *Behind the Lines,* cartoons by Tony Auth (Houghton Mifflin, 1977).

INVITATIONS

Since tapes played such a key role in Watergate, what better way to invite your guests to the party than by sending a audiotaped invitation? Have someone do a Nixon imitation, and then make sure that somewhere in the tape there is the famous eighteen-minute gap—except here make it more like eighteen seconds.

Here's a sample tape script:

NIXON: I am not a crook! This Watergate thing has been blown way out of proportion. If I've said it once, I've said it a thousand times: We could do that, but it would be wrong. I'll just have to prove it to all these people, once and for all. Have them all show up at

---

July 1—Princess Diana's Birthday

This is an excellent date for the Royal Scandals Party. Alternatively, make it a Fleet Street Party, with all the guests coming as tabloid reporters, complete with their own version of the latest Charles/Diana gossip.

[Place] at [Time] on [Date]. And make sure they know
. . . GAP . . . because that's critical!

If you're not into audio, just fill an envelope with lots of
shredded paper, leaving some larger shreds, on which you write
all the critical information.

DECOR

Remember that Watergate was about covert operations. So hide
microphones in the plants, place wires in the potato chip bowl, and
have yards and yards of tapes draped over chairs and pictures.

You just can't have too much fake money or too many shredded documents for this party! Have bowls of them alongside the
food, and add canceled checks, made payable to "The Plumbers."

Since this party is all about political scandal, think about
adding some patriotic decorations. Many fabric stores sell American flag material for about $2.00 a yard. Drape it over the win-
dows and around the food table. Also think about ordering some
patriotic favors and decorations (available from the Beistle Company; see page 134). Options include flags, a constitution cutout,
a "Let Freedom Ring" banner, several different patriotic garlands,
and cutouts of Washington and Lincoln.

You also may want to bring back a few of the more memorable quotes by making posters. These could include:

I AM NOT A CROOK.—Richard Nixon
WHEN YOU'VE GOT THEM BY THE BALLS, THEIR HEARTS AND MINDS
WILL FOLLOW.—a favorite saying of Chuck Colson
TELL KATIE GRAHAM SHE'S GOING TO GET HER TIT CAUGHT IN A BIG
RINGER IF THAT'S PUBLISHED.—John Mitchell
And, of course, the classic: NIXON'S THE ONE.

No Watergate Party will be complete without a "G. Gordon
Liddy Memorial Candle," in honor of the man who was known to

have held his hand over a flame until his flesh burned. When asked how he did it, he responded, "The trick is not minding."

CHARACTERS

Here, more than any other theme party, it is essential that you come as a specific character. Pick one of the following, or add one of your own. For better or worse, there is a large cast from which to choose.

- Richard "Tricky Dick" Nixon. You all know what to do here. Helpful hint: Keep those shoulders hunched. If you think you'd make a good Ed Sullivan at a TV theme party, you'll be a shoo-in for Richard Nixon. And remember to ask Henry Kissinger to kneel before the portrait of Lincoln.
- Pat Nixon. Ever faithful, ever quiet Pat (may she rest in peace) is a good character to play if you're not into heavy conversation but enjoy your martinis.
- Julie Nixon Eisenhower (with or without the faithful David Eisenhower, who could be dressed as Howdy Doody). A Dick Nixon cheerleader's costume would be a nice touch.
- Charles "Chuck" Colson. Special counsel to the president and White House "hatchet man." He should be carrying a paper bag labeled "Dirty Tricks." A paunch, black-rimmed glasses, and the mandatory tie and white shirt are needed. If you want to come as a post-Watergate, "born again" Colson, make sure you're carrying a Bible.

July 19—Women's Convention Anniversary

This day marks the anniversary of a convention organized by Lucretia Mott and Elizabeth Cady Stanton in Seneca Falls, New York, in 1848. Susan B. Anthony attended, and topics of discussion included the vote, property rights, and divorce. Consider staging a Women-Only Party or a Politically Correct Party.

- G. Gordon Liddy. Considering that he served four and a half years in jail, you may want to come in prison garb. Remember, if you come as Liddy you're coming as the prince of self-inflicted torture, so have lots of cigarette burns on your arms. Surely the craziest—if not necessarily the brightest—conspirator. If you want some current tips, tune in to Liddy's talk radio show, which—believe it or not—won the 1995 Freedom of Speech Award by The National Association of Radio Talk Show Hosts. You figure!

- Dorothy Hunt. Was her death in an airplane crash an accident or was she too hot to handle? When Flight 553 from Washington to Chicago went down on December 8, 1972, it was the end of Dorothy Hunt, wife of Watergate burglar and former CIA operative E. Howard Hunt. So we'll never know why she agreed to be a "bagwoman" for the conspirators, or why she was carrying $10,000 in $100 bills on the fateful flight. Think about coming as her ghost. Maybe then some questions will finally be answered.

- Martha Mitchell. What would Watergate be without Martha? The death of this second Watergate wife will always leave us wondering whether Martha was a raving lunatic, a drunk, or a savvy observer, trying to save her man. In any case, Martha will add a touch of color and gaudiness to this conservative crowd. If you come as Martha, make sure that you carry a telephone with you—for those late-night "tell-all" calls to reporters.

- John Mitchell. Forgive him his crude remarks about Katharine Graham's anatomy; old John fell on hard times during Watergate. There is a Sad Sack quality to the John

July 30—Arnold Schwarzenegger's Birthday

The living legend from Austria was born on this date in 1947. Why not throw a Conan or Terminator Party? For true Arnie fans, rent his first Hercules film and determine whether it was dubbed, or did his English just get worse in later years?

Mitchell of Watergate. If only he could have guessed! Early retirement would have looked pretty good.

- H. R. Haldeman. That crewcut was just too much in 1972! Nixon's chief of staff and ultimate White House power broker was as hard as nails. Think about carrying a bullwhip. Tip: Consult *The Haldeman Diaries: Inside the Nixon White House* (Berkley Books, 1995) for some nice extra touches.

- John Ehrlichman. Former counsel and close aide to Nixon, Ehrlichman was Tweedledum to Haldeman's Tweedledee. Known as the Berlin Wall, Hans and Fritz, or Herdleman and Erdleman, these two dated back to their days at U.C.L.A. So if you can't bear to come as Ehrlichman in his boring dark suit, why not don a U.C.L.A. sweatshirt?

- John and Maureen Dean. This look is easy. John, White House counsel and the first White House insider to cooperate with the prosecution, looks like he wrote *The Preppy Handbook*. The horn-rimmed glasses are a must. Mo Dean looks like she stepped out of *Vogue*, with tied-back blond hair and designer clothes. No frugal frump here!

- Rose Mary Woods. If it wasn't for the eighteen-minute gap in a key Watergate tape, would anybody know Rose Mary Woods? But here she is, etched in Watergate history because this loyal, red-headed personal secretary to Nixon took responsibility for the famous erasure. Clearly, if you come as Woods, carry a Dictaphone machine and an instruction manual. You also should spend the evening at Nixon's beck and call.

- Judge Sirica. Without his black judicial robe, this chief judge for the U.S. District Court for the District of Columbia looks as if he could have had a part in *The Godfather*. A key here (other than the robes) would be Brezhnev-like bushy eyebrows.

- Bob Woodward and Carl Bernstein, the *Washington Post* reporters who ferreted out the Watergate story. Just wear your typical 1972 garb and carry a steno pad in your back pocket. In real life they don't look as good as Robert Red-ford and Dustin Hoffman, who played the parts in the movie. So what else is new?

- Deep Throat. We'll never know the identity of the high-level informer who met Bob Woodward in an out-of-the-way garage at odd hours to feed the reporter critical information that would help to bring down Richard Nixon. So take some liberties here. You could wear a dark coat, a black fedora pulled over your eyes, and shades. Or you could concoct something more exotic.
- Frank Wills. Last, but certainly not least, think about coming as the $80-a-week General Security Service guard who just happened to notice some tape on a door at the Watergate complex. The rest, as the saying goes, is history.

MUSIC

Lots and lots of '60s music for this bash. Didn't you always want to see Dick Nixon "get down" to the music of The Band or The Grateful Dead? Here is some suggested music:

"Ain't No Sunshine" by Bill Withers
"Family Affair" by Sly and the Family Stone
"Lonely Days" by The Bee Gees
"Neither One of Us (Wants to Be the First to Say Good-bye)" by Gladys Knight & The Pips—a great duo for Ehrlichman and Haldeman to perform
"What's Going On" by Marvin Gaye
"Will It Go Round in Circles" by Billy Preston

ACTIVITIES

Test your Watergate memory with a game of Watergate hangman. Get some big pieces of poster board or a giant pad. Then try to stump the crowd with some of the more obscure Watergate names. Some could include:

Magruder
Rebozo
Ruckelshaus
Segretti

Who are these men? Answers: (1) deputy director, White House communications; (2) "Bebe"—the millionaire businessman and longtime Nixon friend; (3) deputy attorney general (casualty of the "Saturday Night Massacre"; (4) Dirty trickster: lawyer hired to disrupt the Democratic campaign.

You also could have a Watergate scavenger hunt. A few sug-

Backdrop for the Watergate Party.
See instructions on page 132.

gestions to get you going are: a plunger (for the plumbers, of course), a copy of *Blind Ambition*, any photograph of Nixon, and any written text that has the phrase "expletive deleted."

PRIZES

Make up bookmarks or even T-shirts with some of the famous Watergate quotes. (See page 72.) Replicas of Nixon campaign buttons would also be a nice touch.

Since this crowd is clever and quick with words (how else could they manage such an elaborate cover-up?) try some limericks. Go around the room, and have each person add a line based on his or her character. For example:

Guest 1: There once was a pres. named Dickie
Guest 2: Whose tactics were really quite tricky
Guest 3: Unfortunately for him
Guest 4: His cover wore thin
Guest 5: And he left feeling quite icky.

THE SCANDALS PARTY

If you've ever been tempted by the *National Enquirer* while waiting on the checkout line at the grocery store or found yourself taking a peek at *People*'s latest dirt on the royal family, then you are a prime candidate for the Scandals Party.

Let's face it, we are a nation obsessed with gossip. For better or worse, we are attracted like bees to nectar by the love affairs, true confessions, and indiscretions of our favorite Hollywood stars, politicians, and athletes.

Did Michael Jackson really try to buy the remains of the Elephant Man? And who has been sucking the toes of the Duchess of

AUGUST

August 7—Halfway Point of Summer

Check the *Farmer's Almanac* for exact time.

York? Let your fantasies go wild and dress up as your favorite scandalous figures.

INVITATIONS

Since gossip is so key to scandals, think about a self-mailer (see page 129), using a "confidential" sticker (available at any office supply store) to seal the letter. The front of the mailer should say:

Did you hear . . .

and the message continues inside:

that there is going to be the scandal party of the decade? And you're invited! People will gossip unless you come as a subject of scandal (living or dead, fictitious or real).

[Time, Place, Date]

And don't dare to come without an RSVP.

[Number]

August 16—Anniversary of Elvis Presley's Death

Pay tribute to the King, who passed away at 3:30 P.M. on this date in 1977. Consider a full-blown Elvis Party, complete with a large Cadillac backdrop and lots of tight pants and dancing to his greatest hits. For a more subdued memorial, invite a few friends in and rent a classic Elvis film, such as *Viva Las Vegas* or *Jailhouse Rock*.

DECOR

My preference to set the mood of the party would be cheap gossip. Paper the walls with some classic headlines from the *National Enquirer* and other tabloids. Buy a life-size cutout of Marilyn Monroe (see pages 134–35) and paste on a sign DID SHE DO IT WITH BOBBY AND JOHN?

Also find a large poster of Prince Charles and place a sign over it: WHY DID THIS MAN WANT TO BE A TAMPAX?

And don't forget the politicians. Get a picture of a yacht and place a sign on it: IT AIN'T THE LOVE BOAT, IT'S MONKEY BUSINESS.

Scatter the room with Kitty Kelley books and other unauthorized biographies of the stars.

COSTUMES

Here are some suggestions:

From the World of Entertainment:

- Woody Allen and Mia Farrow (a third guest could always prove that three's a crowd by coming as Soon-Yi Previn)
- Elizabeth Taylor and Richard Burton
- Elizabeth Taylor and Malcolm Forbes
- Elizabeth Taylor and Michael Jackson
- Marilyn Monroe and one of the Kennedys
- Truman Capote (the man was a walking scandal all by himself)
- Joan Crawford (with or without instruments of cruelty)
- Michael Jackson and Lisa Marie Presley (with or without a young boy in tow)

Britain:

Any of the royals will do. Of particular interest would be:

- Princess Diana and Prince Charles (with or without Camilla)
- the Duchess of York, Sarah Ferguson (Fergie), with her most recent toe-nibbler
- Prince Andrew with a soft porn star
- Edward and Mrs. Wallis Simpson (he gave up the throne for her)
- and last, but certainly not least, the Queen and her corgies

Our Nation's Capital:

Mark Twain once said that "There is no distinctly native American criminal class except for Congress." Whether we agree with Twain or not, our distinguished leaders in Washington have given us a number of choice scandals from which to choose:

- Wilbur Mills (D-Arkansas, chairman of the House Ways and Means Committee) and stripper Fanne Foxe (also known as the Argentina Firecracker). Clearly, her costume will be a lot more fun than his conservative dark suit, but accessories (fifths of vodka and burlesque props) will make all the difference here.
- Congressman Wayne Hayes and Liz Ray, the secretary who "couldn't type." Liz, as a former Miss Virginia, could come decked as a beauty pageant contestant, complete with swimsuit and sash, or in her office garb, with a "How to Type" manual.
- Billygate: If it had stopped with Billy Beer, things might have been okay for the wayward brother of Jimmy Carter, the president who lusted only in his heart. But Billy Carter was forced to register as a foreign agent after accepting a $220,000 "loan" from the Libyan government. Blue jeans,

geeky black-rimmed glasses, a pillow in the gut, and a six-pack are necessities for this character.

- Spiro Agnew. While in office, Agnew resigned after it was revealed that he was under investigation in Maryland for as many as fifty possible violations of federal bribery, extortion, conspiracy, and tax laws. Come as Spiro with pockets full of cash. Just in case you think people won't recognize you, you could wear a sign SPIRO WHO?

- Bill Clinton and Gennifer Flowers, who should be carrying a bag of her famous "love tapes" from her alleged twelve-year affair with the then-governor of Arkansas. Hillary (carrying her own Whitewater papers) is an optional addition.

The Criminal Element:

> Lizzie Borden took an ax
> and gave her mother forty whacks.
> And when she saw what she had done . . .
> She gave her father forty-one!

- Think about coming as the most notorious murder suspect from Fall River, Massachusetts—Lizzie Borden. Standard Victorian dress, with one very important addition: an ax. You may consider adding red paint to the blade.

- Jack the Ripper: Was he a member of the royal household, a prominent London physician, or just a run-of-the-mill psycho? In any case, old Jack created quite a scandal when

August 29—Ingrid Bergman's Birthday

Honor one of the all-time best leading ladies with a *Casablanca* Party. Decorate your home as Rick's American Café, have "As Time Goes By" playing as background music when guests arrive, and hunt for the stolen letters of transit—only please, don't hide them in the piano!

he stalked London's East End slums in the late 1800s. A black cape and top hat would do nicely, along with the weapon of choice.

- Jeffrey Dahmer: Just a regular-looking guy, except that he stored dismembered heads and human meat in his refrigerator. Suggested props would be an electric saw or the rubber anatomically correct "Dead Leg," available from the Klutz Flying Apparatus Catalogue. (See page 139.)
- The Menendez Brothers: Erik and Lyle claimed to be abused children, but why the initial cover-up?

Backdrop for the Scandals Party.
See instructions on page 132.

Tabloid Stars Worth Considering:

- O. J. Simpson and the entire cast of characters who were involved in the trial. These include: the Dream Team (Robert Shapiro, F. Lee Bailey, Johnnie Cochran, Jr., and Alan Dershowitz; Al Cowlings (carrying the keys to the Bronco); Marcia Clark; Detective Mark Fuhrman; Judge Lance Ito; and, of course, Brian (Kato) Kaelin, the house-guest longing for his fifteen minutes of fame.
- Lorena and John Wayne Bobbitt (with or without his "member")
- Tonya Harding and company (former husband Jeff Gillooly [a.k.a. Stone] and "bodyguard" Shawn Eckardt). Nancy "Why me?" Kerrigan would be a nice addition.
- Amy Fisher and Joey Buttafuoco: The Long Island Lolita and the less-than-attractive object of her affection.
- Imelda Marcos: Nothing hard here. Shoes, shoes, and more shoes. Bring a suitcase full.
- Michael Milken: Come as the junk bond king with a crown made of bogus bonds or Monopoly money. Ticker tape accessories would be a nice addition.
- Tammy Faye and Jim Bakker: The makeup needs to be so thick that you could cut it with a knife (don't get any ideas, Ripper), and waterproof mascara is a must. Jim can be carrying a Bible, with a condom as a bookmark.
- The Mayflower Madam or Heidi Fleiss, "madam to the stars," could come with a very tasteful—and revealing— black book.

Characters from Fiction:

- Emma Bovary or Anna Karenina give you a nice opportunity to flaunt some stunning period costuming.
- If colonial New England appeals to you, think about coming as Hester Prynne (make that scarlet letter big) and the Reverend (it takes two to tango) Dimmesdale.

MUSIC

Suggest that each of your scandalous characters brings an appropriate recording. You may take turns playing these, with an appropriate introduction from the guest. Or if the crowd is up for it, each character could perform a number. Here are some suggestions:

Jim Bakker: "My Prayer" by The Platters

Jeffrey Dahmer: "Just My Imagination (Running Away with Me)" by The Temptations or "The Purple People Eater" by Sheb Wooley

Fergie: "Do That to Me One More Time" by The Captain & Tennille

Amy Fisher: "Bad Girls" by Donna Summer

Fanne Foxe: "The Stripper" by David Rose

Imelda Marcos: "These Boots Are Made for Walking" by Nancy Sinatra or "Blue Suede Shoes" by Elvis

Wilbur Mills: "Baby Let Me Bang Your Box" by numerous artists

Jimmy Swaggart: "Papa Don't Preach" by Madonna

ACTIVITIES

Tabloid Headline Charades: Stock up on some good trash reading from your local supermarket and newsstand, and then divide up into two teams and select headlines for a charades competition.

August 30—The First *Late Show With David Letterman* broadcast on CBS

Celebrate Dave's newfound status (and fortune) with a Late Show Party. Tell each guest to be prepared with a Stupid Human or Stupid Pet Trick. And make sure you have at least one Top Ten list—for example, the top-ten reasons why this party is crazy.

DANCING

This is a group of live wires, so get them up and dancing. It wouldn't surprise me to see Donald Trump dancing with "hot" Anna Karenina, or Prince Charles tapping his toes next to Fanne Foxe. But tell me this: Who will dance with Jeffrey Dahmer?

PRIZES

Copies of the most recent *National Enquirer, Star,* or *Globe* are always appropriate for a Scandals Party.

Another idea would be a copy of Kitty Kelley's most recent unauthorized biography or O.J.'s Legal Pad, fabricated by Henry Beard & John Boswell (Villard Books, 1995).

For the graft and corruption crowd, hand out Money Memo Pads (Sarsaparilla, 5711 Washington Street, West New York, NJ 07093).

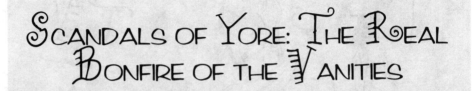

Scandals of Yore: The Real Bonfire of the Vanities

Scandals are certainly nothing new. In fact, during medieval times, scandals were rampant. Not surprisingly, this was particularly so in Italy. With regularity, impassioned church zealots would try to reform the sexual promiscuity and lavish indulgences of the clergy and lay population alike.

It wasn't particularly shocking, therefore, when, in the late 1490s, Girolamo Savonarola, an impassioned reformer, took control of Florence when the powerful Medici family fell from power. He encouraged "bonfires of vanities," where citizens were asked to destroy works of art, books, and other "pagan" possessions. The good people of Florence responded.

But it appears their hearts weren't really in it. It was, they decided, too much of a sacrifice. So the year after the bonfires, the citizens turned on Savonarola. He was arrested, tortured, and burned as a heretic.

The moral of the story: Don't play with fire unless you're willing to be burned.

'50s/'60s/'70s

TV

*L*assie, *Fury, Sea Hunt, Rin Tin Tin, The Lone Ranger, Zorro, Davy Crockett,* and yes, even *Howdy Doody* dominated my child-hood. To me, television was truly a wonder, and there was no such thing as too much, or bad, TV.

One year I had the worst attendance record at P.S. 193. But what I missed in class, I more than made up for by sitting in front

SEPTEMBER

September 8—Anniversary of the First *Star Trek* Show

For Trekkies, this can be a trip down memory lane for the cult show that was first broadcast in 1966. What better way to honor Captain Kirk and the *Enterprise* crew than to boldly go where no party has gone before?

of the boob tube watching *Play Your Hunch, Concentration, Jeopardy!* (before the big electronic board), *What's My Line, Treasure Hunt, Truth or Consequences,* and *The Price Is Right.*

Considering this fascination, it wasn't surprising that a few years ago we decided to bring back the golden days of television by throwing a TV Theme Party.

INVITATIONS

Since this party cries out for an audio invitation, consider this:

Re-create the opening of *Mission Impossible.* Record the opening theme (available on *Television's Greatest Hits,* Tee Vee Toons, 220 Central Park South, NY, NY 10019), fade out the music, and then record a voice-over: "Your mission, should you decide to accept it, is [to attend a TV Theme Party at Ted and Sarah's on Saturday, October 9, at 8:00 P.M. You must come disguised as a famous television character, and RSVP by September 28.] Should you or any member of your M.I. force be captured, the secretary will disavow any knowledge of your existence. This tape will self-destruct in five seconds." After a five-second gap, the voice comes on again: "They just don't make these tapes like they used to, but the invitation still stands!" Close with a repeat of the theme song.

The good part about this is that you don't need to be a rocket scientist to handle the technology—after all, you're not going for a Grammy. Just take any tape recorder and hold it up to a stereo speaker to record the theme song, then lower the volume and talk into the tape recorder microphone. Then make multiple copies using a boom box.

September 15—Agatha Christie's Birthday

Why not celebrate Dame Agatha's birth (1890) with a mystery party. Guests could come as either Hercule Poirot or Jane Marple.

DECOR

Have at least one life-size cardboard cutout from the *Starship Enterprise* at the party—preferably greeting guests at the front door. Then decorate the walls with re-creations of some of the old bumper stickers: DOCTOR KILDARE IS A DOLL, or I'VE GOT A CASE ON BEN CASEY.

Make a giant game board for *Jeopardy!* (see activities for its use later in the party, page 95), and place signs at various places in the house: 2,000 MILES TO THE PONDEROSA, or BEAM ME UP, SCOTTY. Other signs could read: YOU'RE GOING TO THE MOON, ALICE; KOOKIE, LEND ME YOUR COMB; or the lines made famous by Maxwell Smart, WOULD YOU BELIEVE? and SORRY ABOUT THAT, CHIEF.

Tape some old TV standards and have them playing (no sound, please) on the VCR.

COSTUMES

Since you remain in character all night, make sure you pick someone that you're comfortable playing. You might get a big reaction if you come as Clarabell from *Howdy Doody*, but honking your horn all night in lieu of conversation might get tiresome—not to mention your host's reaction to your spraying seltzer at the other guests. In the same way, Lassie, Fury, Rin Tin Tin, or Flipper are of limited interest. Mr. Ed, the talking horse, however, has distinct possibilities.

Here are some suggestions.

Comedies

Come as any member of the cast of the *Beverly Hillbillies*, Ralph and Alice Kramden from *The Honeymooners* (two other friends can come as Trixie and Ed Norton), Lucy and Ricky Ricardo (with Fred and Ethel Mertz) from *I Love Lucy*, Maynard G. Krebbs from *Dobie Gillis*, The Flying Nun, the Fonz from *Happy*

Days, members of the Addams or Munster families, or Jeannie from *I Dream of Jeannie*. A whole group of friends can come as the crowd from the 4077th Mobile Army Surgical Hospital (*M*A*S*H*), or you could come solo as Corporal Klinger—in drag, of course.

If you would like to extend the military theme, go back to the 1950s with Sergeant Bilko and his sidekick Doberman.

Backdrop for '50s/'60s/'70s TV Party.
See instructions on page 132.

Westerns

Recycle your costumes from the Wagons Ho Party and come as Paladin from *Have Gun Will Travel* (very similar to Wilson from *Shane*, when you come to think of it—dressed all in black, but carrying a business card with a knight from a chess game—very profound for the late 1950s). There is always the crew from *Bo-*

nanza (no parts for women, however, unless you cross-dress as Hop Sing, the Chinese cook), and my personal favorites: Flint McCullough (Robert Horton), the too-sexy scout from *Wagon Train*, and Rowdy Yates (a very young Clint Eastwood) from *Rawhide*.

Doctor Shows

As far as I'm concerned, there are only two to consider: *Dr. Kildare* and *Ben Casey*. An interesting character would be Dr. Zorba, Ben's mentor. He's easy to play: just recycle an Albert Einstein wig and put on a white lab coat.

Police Shows

Re-create Theo Kojak by coming bald and sucking a lollipop, or take an entirely funky route by playing Gunther Toody and Francis Muldoon from *Car 54, Where Are You?* If you go for deadpan, think about Eliot Ness from *The Untouchables* or Joe Friday from *Dragnet*. Consider the too-cool *Mod Squad* from the late 1960s, with three swinging undercover cops: Pete, from a wealthy white family; Julie, a poor white from a broken home; and Linc, a militant black, busted during a race riot.

Espionage

If you ever owned a button that said ALL THE WAY WITH ILLYA K or FLUSH THRUSH, then you've found your characters: Illya Kuryakin or Napoleon Solo from *The Man from U.N.C.L.E.* If you go for less subtle humor, Maxwell Smart and 99 from *Get Smart* are possibilities. There is also the *Mission: Impossible* crew, or Alexander "Scotty" Scott (Bill Cosby) and Kelly Robinson (Robert Culp) from *I Spy*.

September 20—Battle of the Sexes Day

For those of you old enough to remember, on this day in 1973 Bobby Riggs challenged Billie Jean King to the second Battle of the Sexes on the tennis court. Billie Jean won in straight sets. Celebrate with a Battle of the Sexes Party—complete with organized games that pit the women against the men.

Space Adventures

It would seem unlikely that anyone could host a TV Party and not have one member of the *Star Trek* crew attend, so bring out those Vulcan ears. And don't forget *Lost in Space*, where Lassie's mom (June Lockhart) and fellow crew members spent three years (1965–1968) trying to find a way home. No ET, they couldn't just phone.

ACTIVITIES

The TV Theme Song Quiz

I have a very annoying habit. When I can't fall asleep, I hum old TV theme songs. In my weaker moments I admit that having to listen to an off-key rendition of the theme from *I Love Lucy* can become tiresome at 2:00 A.M. But it would be appropriate—and fun—to test your guessing skills at the TV Party.

Fortunately, there are now compact discs and tapes out with fantastic anthologies of TV theme songs. (For example, *Television's Greatest Hits*—see page 91 for details.) So give your guests a score sheet, pick out a mix of the obvious (so the less obsessive TV watchers won't come up with a goose egg), and take the Theme Song Quiz.

An ideal gift for the winner would be a copy of *The TV Theme Song Sing-Along Song Book* by John Javna (St. Martin's Press, 1984) $6.95. or Volume 2 (St. Martin's Press, 1985) $5.95.

Re-create a Favorite Quiz Show

Jeopardy!

Invite one or two friends over a week or two before the party and construct your own *Jeopardy!* board. For the purposes of the party, don't bother with Double Jeopardy—it will take too long. After one round, go right into Final Jeopardy. The winner could be given the *Jeopardy!* game, the *Jeopardy!* book, or the *Jeopardy!* calendar.

The Price Is Right

Confession: Whenever I make a bet on anything that involves a number as the answer (and I do this a lot), I always add: *Price Is Right* rules. For those who have lived in a cave for the past thirty years, with *Price Is Right* rules, the one who gets closest without going over wins.

Once everyone is in agreement on the rules, pick three contestants for each bidding item. But instead of guessing the price of a washer and dryer (boring!), bring out more creative things: a dozen novelty condoms, the Sexy Charades game (from Ivory Tower), a box of Depends, or a bottle of Geritol. Winners get to keep the item on which they bid successfully. It might be appropriate to open some of the prizes at the party—others must wait until you get home.

The Gong Show

If your crowd tends to get rowdy, a sure winner would be a mini *Gong Show*. This one is a no-brainer. Just have your less inhibited friends give an impromptu performance, and when it gets so bad that it is downright embarrassing, "gong" them. A large pan and spoon will do the job.

Other game show re-creations could include *Beat the Clock*, *Let's Make a Deal*, or *Queen for a Day* (just make sure that you've got that nice crown and an applause meter).

PRIZES

Small favors could include temporary *Flintstone* tattoos or plastic figures, *Batman* dolls, TV theme song CDs or tapes, or TV books, such as *The TV Guide TV Book* by Ed Weiner and the editors of *TV Guide* (Harper Perennial, 1992) $9.95 or *The TV Almanac* (Macmillan, 1994) $10.00.

For our TV Party, three of us came as the Flintstones (to be exact, two came as Wilma and Fred Flintstone and one as Barney Rubble).

As the shortest member of our threesome (with the physique that could most readily pass for a fire hydrant), I was chosen to play Barney. All I needed was a caveman outfit, made out of fake fur, and a wig. Wilma looked kind of spiffy with the big bone in her hair, Fred looked dapper carrying his stone (in reality, papier-mâché) bowling ball, and I looked plain stupid in my little fur suit.

While we did get a good laugh from the crowd, we lost the costume contest to two friends who could have doubled for Lucy and Ricky. But it didn't end there.

It turned out that others were secretly eyeing my fake-fur caveman outfit, and it soon became much sought after. First it was borrowed for Halloween and then for a Wild Things Party. The last time I lent it to a friend who wanted to wear it for a video performance. This friend, however, was close to a foot taller than I am and had difficulty getting into this rather skimpy costume. It went on without too much difficulty, but getting it off was an entirely different matter. It just stuck like glue. No matter how hard we pulled, it wouldn't budge. Eventually we managed to pry it off—without the embarrassment of calling the fire department—but, after that, the old cave suit never had quite the same appeal.

THE COLD WAR PARTY

❋

It was an era of good guys and bad guys. Superpowers. Khrushchev banging his shoe at the U.N. A Commie around every corner. It seems silly now, but we took our air raid shelter drills very seriously at P.S. 193. But when you think about it, what good would it do if we were in the hall rather than our classrooms when an atomic bomb hit? Never mind. Mrs. Silverman could never explain it either.

Red mania was everywhere—so much so that in 1959, newlyweds in Miami set a record for the longest time spent in a bomb

---

September 24—F. Scott Fitzgerald's Birthday

Create flapper costumes and re-create the Roaring '20s with the Speakeasy Party. Go ahead and hang some fringe on those miniskirts, and put some colorful feathers in those tennis sweatbands!

shelter. It seems that they spent their entire two-week honeymoon twelve feet under. To each his own.

It was also the era of Levittowns in suburbia, poodle skirts, crewcuts, and saddle shoes. Hopalong Cassidy, Gene Autry, and Roy Rogers and Dale Evans were our TV heros.

It's all history now. But we thought it would be fun to bring back the era (and all its silliness and paranoia) in a Cold War Party.

INVITATIONS

Remember, this is the time of the House Un-American Activities hearings. Everyone and his or her brother were being called upon to testify before Senator Joseph McCarthy. So why not send out your invitations as subpoenas in official-looking envelopes? (If you want to really get serious, send them by registered mail.) Then make a fake letterhead from the House Un-American Activities Committee and word the invitation something like this:

```
                               DATE, 1951

You, [NAME], are being subpoenaed to
appear before the House Un-American
Activities Committee at [TIME], [DATE], at
[ADDRESS]. Come in period dress, or even
better, as a historic figure from the time.

                      RSVP before [DATE].
```

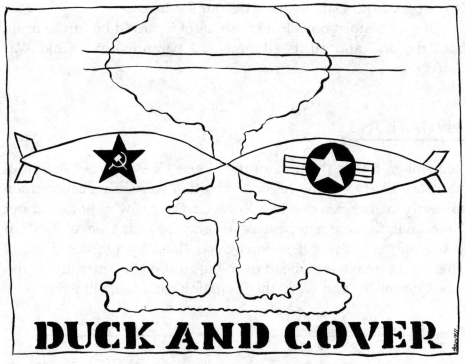

DUCK AND COVER

Backdrop for the Cold War Party.
See instructions on page 132.

DECOR

Think about decorating in bomb shelter motif. Pull down all the window shades and have lots of canned goods everywhere. (Spam would be a nice '50s touch.)

Make replicas of the yellow civil defense signs, and hang several around the room. Also, make some posters that say BETTER DEAD THAN RED or DUCK AND COVER.

You may consider ordering some radiation warning labels or radiation decontaminant from a scientific supply company.

If you want to get really macabre, make a big mushroom cloud.

You should also have lots of Tupperware around. In fact, why not serve all your food in Tupperware?

OCTOBER

The entire month of October is National Pizza Month. Order out and have a few friends in for some pies—no anchovies, please! Or, if you are up for a do-it-yourself dinner, have a Make Your Own Pizza Party. If you aren't into taking the time to make homemade dough, buy Boboli bread and lots of different toppings, and let your friends test their creativity. (Hint: You can use peppers, pepperoni, or olives to create customized messages or "pictures" on the pizzas.)

COSTUMES

You could, of course, just come in standard '50s dress, but it would be so much more fun for everyone to come as historic figures—and there is no shortage of great characters.

From the Commie side, you have Nikita Khrushchev (who can be wearing two shoes, or just wearing one and carrying the other); Castro, complete with beard, cigar, and army fatigues; and Mao, wearing his worker's jacket and cap. Mrs. Mao could come in a matching costume.

And what would a Cold War Party be without a younger Richard Nixon? Other Americans could include Francis Gary Powers, in his jumpsuit, after his U-2 spy plane was shot down over the Soviet Union; Robert J. Oppenheimer, scholarly with a knit vest, a jacket with suede patches on the elbows, and pipe; or Julius and Ethel Rosenberg. And what would the Cold War be without General Douglas MacArthur, complete with bomber jacket and aviator sunglasses?

A well-endowed Kate Smith, singing "God Bless America," would make a wonderful addition. The party just wouldn't be complete without Senator Joe McCarthy and J. Edgar Hoover (in either a suit or a stunning red dress).

October 10—Spiro Agnew Resigns

Spiro Theodore Agnew, the second person to resign from the vice-presidency of the United States, did so on this day in 1973. A prize should be given to the guest who can name the first vice-president to resign. [Answer: John C. Calhoun] To celebrate this historic date, throw a Nolo Contendere or a Remember Agnew Party. Sixties dress required.

MUSIC

To provide appropriate music, buy the tape of *Atomic Cafe* (Rounder Records), which includes such cuts as "Atom and Evil," "Atomic Cocktail," "Atomic Love," and other Cold War classics. In addition, consider some of these oldies but goodies:

"Dear Ivan" by Jimmy Dean
"The End of the World" by Skeeter Davis
"Eve of Destruction" by Barry McGuire
"Guided Missile (Aimed at My Heart)" by The Valadiers
"Hard Rain's A-Gonna Fall" by Bob Dylan
"The Hydrogen Bomb" by Al Rogers and His Rocky Mountain Boys
"Midnight in Moscow" by Kenny Ball and His Jazz Band
"Mr. Khrushchev" by Bo Diddley
"Sh-Boom" by The Chords, inspired by the atomic bomb blast
"Talking World War III Blues" by Bob Dylan
"There's a Star Spangled Banner Waving Somewhere No. 2: The Ballad of Francis Powers" by Red River Dave
"West of the Wall" by Miss Toni Fisher

ACTIVITIES

If you own, or have access to, a home video camera, you can have a lot of fun making your own 1950s propaganda videos. The best way would be to divide the guests into groups of five to six people. Each group should "brainstorm" at the same time, but in different rooms. Then take turns filming in the party room.

The possibilities are limitless: You could do a take-off of the civil defense films of the '50s, create a *National Lampoon*–style bomb shelter comedy, or even a "Debby Does the Bomb Shelter" soft porn spoof.

Use your *Atomic Cafe* tape for background music, or have one of the "actors" lip-sync to one of the catchy Cold War songs.

It's very likely that your crew may get carried away with their newfound creative streak, so make sure to set a time limit (no more than five minutes for the video and a half hour to create this masterpiece). Once all the videos are completed, the whole group should watch and judge the winner.

And whatever you do, don't forget to buy enough video-tapes.

PRIZES

Every guest should be given a door prize: a piece of the Berlin Wall. (In actuality, it can be a piece of everyday rubble with a fancy tag in a plastic sandwich bag.) A bit of German graffiti with a little piece of wire would be a nice touch.

The group that wins the video contest should also be awarded a prize. Consider DUCK AND COVER T-shirts, House Un-American Activity Committee stationery, or FROM THE DESK OF NIKITA KHRUSHCHEV notepads.

OscarNight

*

A Party in Two Parts

This theme party is a guaranteed winner. We've done it nine years in a row, and each year more friends ask to be included. While this party works best for the Oscars, it can also be used for the Grammys, Emmys, Tonys, or any other award celebration.

To prepare, suggested background reading includes *50 Golden Years of Oscar* by Robert Osborn (ESE California, 1979) and *Inside Oscar: The Unofficial History of the Academy Awards* by Mason Wiley and Damien Bona (Ballantine, 1986).

PART I: WATCHING THE SHOW

At around 11:00 P.M., when you have seen one too many glitzy production numbers and had your fill of save-the-world and I'd-especially-like-to-thank-my-dog acceptance speeches, you may wonder why it is that every year you get sucked into watching this extravaganza.

But the fact remains that the Oscars are a cultural phenomenon watched around the world, and if you don't partake, you feel as if you are missing something important.

So invite a group of friends over to watch the Oscars, but make it clear that everyone who attends must participate in a competition. Ballots and "tip sheets" are distributed. (See pages 110–12.) Because voting is taken very seriously, guests are invited to a pizza dinner beforehand, where all recent magazine and newspaper articles on the Oscar picks are available for review. A week or two before Oscar Night, take a trip to your local newsstand and buy one of every magazine that features Oscar picks and gossip. (Past best bets have been *TV Guide,* the local newspaper, *Entertainment Weekly,* and *Premiere.*)

Helpful Hint: In seeking out various opinions on possible winners, vote opposite the choices of Siskel and Ebert in all but the most obvious categories. Two thumbs up to their colorful reviews, but two major thumbs down to their track record on Oscar picks.

COSTUMES

To help get in the mood, suggest that your guests come in Hollywood attire. This can range from glitter and boas to Malibu cool. Shades, inline skates, bright exercise wear, and plunging necklines (for women) or black tie or ascot (for men) are all appropriate.

October 14—National Frump Day

A time for those of us who just don't seem to put ourselves together quite properly to feel good about ourselves. Invite stylish friends over and, for once, be the belle of the ball. It's our party and we'll laugh if we want to. . . .

DECOR

Since your focus will be on the television, you don't need to go overboard. The Oscar backdrop and one or two faux statues will suffice.

PART II: THE WINNER'S REVENGE (THERE IS MORE AT STAKE THAN PRIDE)

To make sure that everyone puts forth his or her best effort—and stays until the end—the guest who gets the highest score on the Oscar ballot becomes Oscar champ for the year. As winner, he or she wins the right to host Oscar Night Party Part II: The Winner's Revenge, a second party that takes place within the next few months.

It's understood from the start that all Oscar Night participants are morally obligated to partake in Oscar Night Party II. For this evening, the winner selects a movie of his or her choice, knowing that there will be a captive audience.

When the winner has selected the night for the viewing and the film to be shown, invitations are mailed to all Oscar Night participants. While giving the date and location, the invitation does not give away the name of the movie, which remains a secret until the evening of the screening.

Again, Hollywood attire should be requested. And you should recycle any decorations that you used on Oscar Night.

Once all guests are gathered, the lights are dimmed and the VCR is turned on. But before the feature film begins, a homemade video introduction, starring the winner, is shown. (While the winner-host could imitate the classy style of Alastair Cooke on *Masterpiece Theatre,* in our experience the host more closely resembles a weirdo in shades and a trench coat.) Gradually through the introduction hints are dropped, so by the end, the captive audience knows what they will be watching.

**Backdrop for Oscar Party.
See instructions on page 132.**

October 22—Annette Funicello's Birthday

The perfect date for your Beach Blanket Bingo Party.

A Sampling of Past Films Selected by Oscar Night Winners

- *Amazon Women on the Moon* A very funky comedy, this 1987 film successfully lampoons the 1950 science fiction movies, know-it-all TV movie critics, and local late-night television commercials. The scene with Ed Begley, Jr., playing "The Invisible Man" is priceless.
- *American Graffiti* This 1973 movie was George Lucas's first commercial success. A great '60s nostalgia film, it is worth viewing for the sound track alone.
- *Chinatown* An all-star cast headed up by Jack Nicholson, Faye Dunaway, and John Huston makes this 1974 movie a winner. But the crowd has to pay close attention because the plot twists and turns more than San Francisco's Lombard Street. Not a good choice if the crowd is rowdy.
- *Earth Versus the Flying Saucers* Classic sci-fi, the kind of movie spoofed in *Amazon Women on the Moon*. A camp film for some; for others, a real snoozer.
- *The Producers* Zero Mostel and Gene Wilder are at their best in this 1968 comedy about a scam to produce a sure-fire Broadway flop, *Springtime for Hitler*.
- *Quest for Fire* Unless you enjoy a lot of grunting, leave this so-called comedy on the video store shelf. The viewing crowd was openly hostile the year this film was shown!
- *Some Like It Hot* A 1959 comedy classic. Tony Curtis and Jack Lemmon (in drag) play two musicians who join a female band while on the lam after witnessing a gangland shootout. Marilyn Monroe, as the ukulele-playing Sugar, steals many of the movie's scenes.

Here's a sample of the tip sheet that should be prepared before your guests arrive on Oscar Night. You'll be surprised how quickly you can begin thinking of your friends as thoroughbreds with very distinct characteristics.

Note: Odds will change yearly to reflect the previous year's standings.

Oscar Awards Tip Sheet

Late Afternoon Edition

Contenders	Odds
Ken "Toxic Avenger" Loveday	**2–1**

Gelding. Likes to take an early lead but is easily distracted. Previous behavior in winner's circle has made the betting crowd skeptical. In top form, with strong legs and a strong desire to win. May be the best of the field on a given day. Note: Always runs on Bute.

| **Ellen "Slow and Steady" Hoffman** | **4–1** |

Excellent "place" bet. Out of the famous Sylvia, Ellen keeps a steady pace but has been known to pull up when she finds herself in the lead. Definitely not a mudder—so stay off this filly on a messy track. A steady performer, though, worth a second look.

Joe "Oscar" Ford   4–1

A former stakes contender, this aging stallion still has lots of spirit but lacks staying power. Those remembering his dramatic come-from-behind victories will surely be disappointed by his current form. Still, the old crowd favorite has the potential to dominate a weaker field. Note: May refuse to break if his jockey isn't wearing designer silks.

Diane "Marathon Man" Kelly   12–1

Comfortable on the track, this Massachusetts-bred filly is untested in Oscar competition. Prefers a longer course and heavy traffic. Experience and staying power may work in Diane's favor.

Louise "Play Your Hunches" Farrell   25–1

Fans are surprised that this track veteran remains a maiden after nine years, despite her impressive breeding. While a longshot, some bettors favor her spirited starts and attention to the grandstand. Sloppy track and multiple distractions can only help. Runs best after her groom has slipped a margarita in her water bucket.

Sample Oscar Ballot

Name: _____

**Point
Value**   **Points**

3   Best Picture_____   ____
3   Best Actor_____   ____
3   Best Actress _____   ____
3   Best Supporting Actor _____   ____
3   Best Supporting Actress _____   ____
3   Best Director _____   ____
2   Original Screenplay _____   ____
2   Adapted Screenplay_____   ____
2   Cinematography _____   ____
1   Art Direction _____   ____
1   Costume Design _____   ____
1   Film Editing _____   ____
1   Original Score _____   ____
1   Original Song_____   ____
                                             TOTAL   ____

TIEBREAKER

Movie to Win the Most Oscars:_____

Number Received: _____

Second Tiebreaker: Best Foreign Movie _____

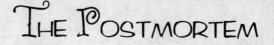

THE POSTMORTEM

It has become a custom for us to do a "postmortem" of the competition the morning after the Oscar presentations. Following in the style of sportswriters, we analyze the previous night's competition in "press releases," which are then faxed to the various competitors. Here is a sample:

FORMER CHAMP HEADED FOR PASTURE?
Trainer Mum as Fans Speculate

**A Special Notice from the
Brookline Racing
Commission**

BROOKLINE, MA, Racing Press—After an unimpressive finish at last night's big Oscar race, Joe "Oscar" Ford's trainers are not talking to the press about this aging stallion's future prospects.

After breaking well and posting a strong first and second furlong, this crowd favorite just ran out of steam when challenged in the stretch by Debbie, the spirited filly from L.A.

When interviewed after the race, Ford's jockey expressed disappointment. "It used to be that I had a lot of horse under me for these big races, but last night my mount was spent long before the finish line."

Trainers of the other horses expressed optimism for next year's outing. "I think the days of Ford dominating this field are over," said the trainer for Ellen "Slow and Steady" Hoffman. "And this is good news for my younger and steadier entry. Yes, next year will be a lot different. Ford will be eating a lot of hay over this one!"

*Note: Names have been changed slightly to protect the participants. You never know when one of them may be tapped for the Supreme Court—and how would they explain this?

New Twists for Old Standards

Here are some suggestions for bringing new life to three "oldies but goodies" parties.

Mardi Gras:

Let the Good Times Roll
✳

First, a disclaimer: Mardi Gras outside New Orleans is just not the real thing. But for those of us who need an excuse to party at the height of the winter doldrums, Mardi Gras offers a great opportunity.

The Mardi Gras carnival season "kickoff" is twelve days after Christmas (Twelfth Night) and continues until the festivities reach a frenzy on Mardi Gras (Fat Tuesday), the day before Ash Wednesday.

To begin your Mardi Gras celebration, have a small group of friends over a week or two prior to Mardi Gras and serve a King Cake (a yeast cake garishly decorated with the traditional Mardi Gras–colored sugar: purple [representing justice], green [representing faith], and gold [representing power]. What makes a King Cake special is that a small plastic baby is hidden somewhere inside the cake before it is baked.

Once the King Cake is served, you and your friends have to

October 24—Stock Market Crash

For those with black humor, celebrate the day when more than 16 million shares were dumped.

keep eating slices until someone gets the baby (and, it is hoped, doesn't swallow it). In true New Orleans tradition—or so I am told—the person who bites into the baby then has to throw the next in a long series of parties.

For our purposes, the person who gets the baby must host a get-together on Mardi Gras night.

Dress in costume—remember to include the mandatory masks—and serve Bourbon Milk Punch and Cajun foods. Keep the music authentic: Dr. John, Professor Longhair, the Neville Brothers, and Irma Thomas are a must.

Decorate in Mardi Gras colors: purple, green, and gold, and have lots of beads, doubloons (fake coins), and assorted trinkets. In New Orleans, these are thrown from the floats. For your party, you'll just have to throw them at each other.

SHORTCUTS

For those not inclined to bake—forgive me, true Mardi Gras aficionados—begin the festivities with a "fake" King Cake. You can buy a Danish ring from a bakery and plant the "baby" through the bottom of the cake. If you want to take it more seriously but still don't want to bake, order the King Cake, along with a host of Mardi Gras trinkets, from one of the following New Orleans bakeries.

Haydel's Bakery, 4037 Jefferson Highway, New Orleans, LA 70121 (504-837-0190) will ship a basic King Cake (serves approximately 35 people) for $25.95. A cake with either German chocolate

October 30—War of the Worlds

On this date in 1938, Orson Welles broadcast H. G. Wells's *War of the Worlds*, and millions of listeners believed that Martians were invading New Jersey. Why not throw an Extraterrestrial Party to celebrate?

or cream cheese filling is 28.95. For an extra $2 they will include a Mardi Gras booklet, trinkets, and beads.

Gambino's Bakery, 3609 Toladano Street, New Orleans, LA 70116 (1-800-GAMBINO)

You will receive a King Cake that serves twelve to sixteen people, and a packet of throws (beads, trinkets, and doubloons) for approximately $30. Options include a Mardi Gras tape ($10.00) and a T-shirt that can be given to the person who finds the baby. The packages are shipped December 15 through Mardi Gras.

McKenzie Bakery, 3847 Desire Parkway, New Orleans, LA 70126 (504-944-8771) offers bargain-rate, plain King Cakes in four sizes from $2.49 to $6.60. Iced medium-sized cakes (serves 14) are $4.49 and filled cakes are $8.79.

Mardi Gras decorations and merchandise can be ordered from:

Accent Annex
1120 South Jefferson Davis Parkway
New Orleans, LA 70125
(504-821-8999)
A free catalog is available.

Las Vegas Night

It's the theme for just about every fund-raiser—for schools, churches, and synagogues—so what could be new and interesting about a Las Vegas Party?

When we threw a Las Vegas Party as a surprise birthday party, we took a different approach. Instead of taking the usual route of giving everyone "gambling money" to use at games of chance, we focused on the other side of Las Vegas—the entertainment.

DECOR

We decorated the house as Caesars Palace, using all the gaudy, colorful props we could find. All the women (except the guest of honor) wore Caesar's togas (in reality, white sheets draped in a semiprovocative way). We tied the togas with gold cord (obtained by the yard at the local fabric store) and made garlands of fake leaves, which we spray-painted gold. The men dressed as dealers—black pants and white shirts. We wore these costumes until it was time to start the floor show, at which point we disappeared one by one into a back room and then emerged as entertainers. The surprise element is an important one here.

THE MAIN EVENT: THE FLOOR SHOW

The elaborate main "show" is put on for an audience of one: the guest of honor. The acts are shoddy at best, but you'll be surprised at how much fun it is to ad-lib a comedy sketch ("He was sooo dumb, he needed to unzip his pants to count to twenty-one!") or pick up a fake mike and lip-sync a crowd-pleasing "I've Got to Be Me." I came as Joan Rivers and did stand-up comedy. It was easier than you might think because you can use books and comedy records for your material.

One guest performed as a very bad ventriloquist. The crowd got rowdy, yelling "Who's the dummy, anyway?" Three others came as Tony Orlando and Dawn. Other possibilities could include Las Vegas legends Wayne Newton, Frank Sinatra, Jay Leno, Don Rickles, or Phyllis Diller.

For the show finale, we made a giant fake birthday cake out of cardboard and tissue paper flowers (à la prom decorations).

One male guest was a good sport and agreed to jump out of the cake wearing only a pair of novelty briefs. (I believe they were red nylon with a telephone appliqué and the words "Out of Order.")

OTHER ACTIVITIES

After the performances, you can try your luck at games of chance. We ending up renting a roulette wheel. Because so many organizations rent gambling equipment for fund-raisers, you probably will find several vendors listed in the yellow pages under "Games and Game Supplies." After explaining to the vendor that ours was a small private party, we were given a break in the price. We paid $75 for the wheel and a large box of chips. (The price included delivery and pickup the following morning.)

We also bought a blackjack felt, and one of the guests filled in as dealer.

All guests were given an equal number of chips, and the one with the most at the end of the evening was awarded a trophy, which we had inscribed at the local trophy store.

Adult Bowling Party

There was a time not too long ago when bowling was considered very déclassé. Sushi was in; bowling was out. However, like bell-bottom pants and wide ties, if you wait around long enough, oldies but goodies will come back into favor. And so has bowling.

Be prepared for some of your friends (who haven't picked up a bowling ball since sixth grade) to turn up their noses. But once they've laced up those too-attractive-to-be-believed bowling shoes (Gosh, you hope that the attendant behind the desk remembered to put the disinfectant powder in after the last person wore them!), you can't help but get into the swing of things.

In New England, we are in the somewhat unique position of having the choice between "candle-pin" bowling (skinny pins) and ten-pin, which we affectionately call "Big Ball." Ten-pin is our personal favorite because it is easier for bowling-challenged individuals like me to get a spare or strike by chance.

The Bowling Party works well for birthdays. You also could throw a Bowling Party to celebrate an anniversary, graduation, or reunion of old friends.

Invitations should encourage guests to find some article of clothing with a bowling motif. I was fortunate enough to be given a beautiful rhinestone bowling pin, and Ken, who grew up in a small town in Pennsylvania, was given a HICKS 'N STICKS bowling shirt. I have also seen bowling ties.

Begin the evening with take-out pizza or Chinese food and then head over to the lanes. Some bowling alleys will reserve lanes. Even if your alley doesn't, it's always a good idea to call ahead to make sure that you're not competing with league activities. If leagues are in play, the attendant will be able to tell you what time the alleys will be free.

Once at the alley, use the honor system and get guests to give you a best guess on their average bowling scores. With our group of friends, this ranges from 65 to 175. To the best of your ability, "handicap" the group and make up two teams. If the teams end up being very lopsided, adjust the handicap after the first game.

NOVEMBER

November 2—Daniel Boone's Birthday

Bring out those old coonskin hats and make a Frontier Party. A good day to throw the Wagons Ho Party. (See pages 3–12.)

PRIZES

You can get small, individual trophies for all participants. (If you go to a trophy store, you will be able to get a real bowling trophy engraved.)

You might want to award a booby prize for the bowler with the worst individual effort. Think about a Bowler's Crying Towel or self-help books. Because I'm a terrible bowler, I have collected quite a number of these self-improvement prizes, including the *Bowler's Guide: Everything Men, Women, and Youngsters Should Know About Playing the Sport of Bowling* (put out by the American Bowling Congress and Women's International Bowling Congress, Greendale, Wisconsin, revised edition, 1976) and *The Secret of Bowling Strikes* by Dawson Taylor (A. S. Barnes and Company, 1960)—collector's items, to be sure.

First Tuesday After First Monday—Election Day

Have friends over to watch the results. Make score sheets and bet on the outcome. Why should Jimmy the Greek have all the action? Have champagne on ice, just in case.

Making It Happen:

Innovative Ideas for Invitations, Decorations, Costumes, and Prizes

INVITATIONS

Your theme party begins with the invitation, so if you want your guests to get into the spirit, here's the place to start.

An offbeat, highly original invitation sends a clear message: This party is going to be something special—and definitely a little wacky. So don't be afraid to do something really original. When we threw a Nerd Party, for example, we wanted to establish the geek theme early, so we sent out invitations in plastic pocket protectors and included a protractor as a favor.

Specific ideas are included for each of the twelve theme parties in the book, but here are a few general guidelines to use as jumping-off points.

November 4—King Tut's Tomb Discovered

Howard Carter found this untouched tomb of the "Boy Pharaoh" in 1922 at Luxor, Egypt. Why not throw a King Tut Party to celebrate? Steve Martin's *King Tut* record is a must, and a backdrop of the Great Pyramids would be perfect. Think about an Egyptian "makeover" activity, where you paint each other's faces with lots of exotic eye makeup. Have fake beards on hand for the would-be pharaohs in the crowd and lots of Ben-Gay for the slaves who have to schlepp all those heavy stones.

INVITATION IDEAS FOR
THE COMPUTER-CHALLENGED

We are now in the age of desktop publishing, where even those who can't draw stick figures can become a Picasso with the right software. But for those of us who have VCRs that continually flash 12:00 and think that MS DOS is married to MR. DOS, there is still hope for creating great invitations without the aid of microchip technology.

There is nothing wrong doing things the old-fashioned way: using rub-on letters, rubber stamps, glitter, feathers, and markers. In fact, you can come up with some really fun, original ideas with supplies that can be found at just about every stationery or art supply store.

The Basics

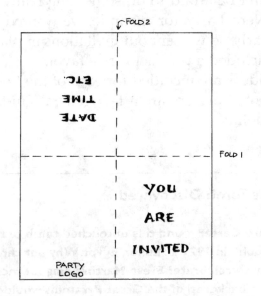

Block out the invitation, and add lettering with rub-on letters. Then photocopy it on colored or special paper. (See page 130.) (Note: Paper of odd weight or size will often jam in the copier, so you may want to run one test copy first.) Once you've made your copies, it's time to test your creativity with rubber stamps, glitter, confetti, stickers, feathers, or anything else you can find. (Only legal substances, please.)

The most simple invitations are "self-mailers." For these, simply print your message on an 8½-by-11-inch sheet of paper, photocopy the number you need, fold the invitations in thirds, and "seal" the invitation with a sticker appropriate for the party.

If you want a more elaborate invitation, fold the paper in half the long way and then in half by width. You will end up with a 5.5-by-4.25-inch card that will fit nicely into a 4¾-by-6½-inch (#6) envelope. Once you've folded it, take a pencil and mark the outside front, outside back, and inside panels lightly in pencil. (Note: See illustration. The tops of the inside and outside panels will be opposite.)

Consider putting some "teaser" on the front cover and the essential information inside. If you want to stamp in black, you can add stamping before the invitation is photocopied. My suggestion, however, would be to add the stamping as a final step, so you can take advantage of colored and sparkle stamp pads.

Rubber Stamps

Today dozens of companies offer an incredibly wide selection of stamps and stamp pads that can be used to make wonderfully creative invitations. Some also offer fabric inks, paper products, and embossing powders and inks.

A partial list includes:

November 7—Nixon's "Last" Press Conference 1962

It looked as if Nixon's political career was over when he lost the governor's race in California to Edmund G. Brown (Jerry Brown's father). Make a banner with Nixon's now-famous quote "You won't have Nixon to kick around anymore. . . ." and commiserate with a few close friends.

Bizarro Rubber Stamps
P.O. Box 16160
Rumford, RI 02916
Catalog: $2.00

Museum of Modern Rubber
187-C Orangethorpe Avenue
Placentia, CA 92670
714-993-3587

Inkadinkado
76 South Street
Boston, MA 02111
617-338-2600
Fax 617-338-5525

Rubber Stamps of America
P.O. Box 567
Saxtons River, VT 05154
1-800-553-5031
Catalog: $2.00

Stamp Francisco
466 Eighth Street
San Francisco, CA 94103
415-252-5975

Paper

Check out your local stationery, card, and art supply stores for paper that is a little out of the ordinary. Be daring with neon, or select a more subtle color that will show off your stamps and glitter well.

For a great selection of mail-order paper, check out the Paper Direct catalog (1-800-A-PAPERS). This catalog offers an incredible variety of papers, ranging from official-looking certificate border papers (perfect for fake diplomas and awards) to fancy paper with confetti embedded in it, to politically correct recycled papers.

An added benefit, for those who are computer-literate, is that all Paper Direct papers can be used in a laser printer. If you're ambitious, you can even buy foils that will switch your standard printing to glitzy metallic—a must for the Great Entertainers Party. Official-looking seals, ribbons, and certificate frames are also available.

Audiotapes

For some parties, it may be more fun to send an audiotape than a printed invitation. Specific examples are given in the Watergate and '50s/'60s/'70s TV chapters. To ensure that the tapes arrive undamaged, buy small padded Jiffy bags for mailing.

Puzzles

Bits and Pieces, a mail-order puzzle company (1-800-544-7297), offers blank puzzles that allow you to write a custom invitation, which you can then break apart and mail. These are also available from some stationery stores. Your guests literally will have to piece together the invitation if they want the essential information of time, place, and date. A set of fifteen blank puzzle notes and envelopes costs $14.95. Small blank puzzles in various shapes, colors, and sizes are often available at specialty paper stores, for between $1.00 and $3.00 per puzzle (with envelopes).

Create-Your-Own Mystery Invitation

If you are hosting a party that involves intrigue, send out a simple invitation that tells your guests to look in the classified ads of your local paper on a specific day, with a clue as to what the ad may say. That's it. Then place the ad in code and leave it to your guests to figure out the specifics.

You also could create your own crossword puzzle invitation, and hope that your friends are sufficiently literate to get the clues. If you're worried, you could emulate the *New York Times* and have a "help number" for those who are desperate.

The "No-Brainer"

If even these relatively simple suggestions seem daunting, don't despair. Here's a suggestion that requires absolutely no artistic input:

November 18—Mickey Mouse's Birthday

M-I-C-K-E-Y M-O-U-S-E! Mickey first appeared on this day in 1928 at the Colony Theatre in New York City, with the showing of *Steamboat Willie*. Ask your guests to come as their favorite Walt Disney characters.

Go to your local card shop and find appropriate humorous postcards to mail out as invitations.

Examples:

Oscar Night: postcards of old movies
Wagons Ho: old cowboy postcards
Politically Incorrect: postcards by cartoonists John Callahan or Gary Larson
Faded Fads: postcards with Barbies

DECOR

THE BACKDROP

The mainstay of your theme party decor will be your backdrop. A specific idea for a backdrop is included for each of the twelve theme parties, but don't feel limited by these suggestions. Use them as jumping-off points. And don't be intimidated because you're not an artist. You're not preparing a canvas for the National Gallery, and no one expects you to be a Rembrandt. Have fun with it!

To make the backdrop, recycle a white, double-sized sheet. If

---

November 30—Abbie Hoffman's Birthday

Born in Worcester, Massachusetts, in 1936, Abbie Hoffman went on to become one of the leaders of the Yippie movement. A defendant in the Chicago Seven trial, he went underground in 1974, surrendered to authorities in 1980, and died in 1989. Remember Abbie with a '60s Party. Attire should include bellbottom pants, granny glasses, and tie-dyed T-shirts. A faux—or even better real—Peter Max poster and Turkish water pipe would provide the correct ambiance.

you don't own one, go out and buy the cheapest one you can find. And don't worry that you'll be viewed as a Plain Jane/Jim by the sales help. Explain to the cashier that it's for a backdrop and that you sleep only on black satin!

To re-create the backdrop, divide the sheet into a 16-square grid (as shown). Enlarge the picture for the backdrop and draw the same grid on that. Then copy the outline of the picture, box by box, using light pencil. When you're satisfied with the result, color in the picture using tempera paints diluted to prevent cracking. And make sure to do this at least a day in advance to allow time for the paints to dry. Once dry, you may want to add accents with crayons, oil sticks, or glitter.

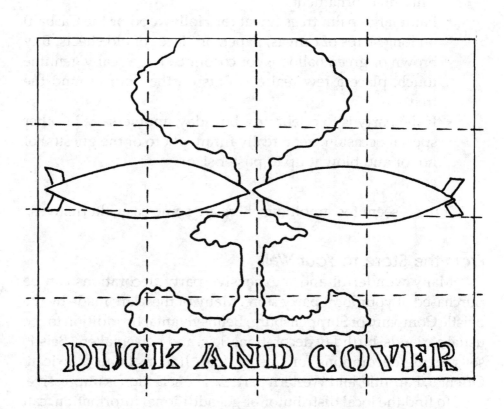

And don't forget about the old Tom Sawyer trick. Invite some friends over. Once they see how much fun it is to paint the backdrop, they'll beg to participate. Let them!

THOSE SPECIAL TOUCHES

Every party benefits from those special little decorating touches. If you have the time, energy, and talent, make your own.

Here are some suggestions.

- Create your own horse, donkey, or any other four-legged critter. Get a sawhorse, make a tail out of a mop, and a head out of poster board rolled into a cylinder that resembles a mini-megaphone. (Add a mane out of a section of the mop.) If you want a gelding, you're all set. If you want a stallion, use balloons or the Styrofoam balls used to make Christmas ornaments.
- Paint large palm trees (great for Hollywood or the Casbah) on long strips of canvas, paper, or pieces of old sheets. Buy brown or green balloons for coconuts. For a really genuine touch, place a few real coconuts on the floor around the tree.
- If the party is to celebrate a birthday, anniversary, or other special occasion, get a really funny photo of the guest(s) of honor and blow it up to poster size.

If these seem too ambitious, here are some easy alternatives.

From the Store to Your Wall

Many wonderful and inexpensive party decorations can be purchased at your local party store. Many of these are made by the Beistle Company of Shippensburg, Pennsylvania. In addition to the usual garlands, birthday decorations, leis, and noisemakers, Beistle sells theme decorations for Casino, '50s, Italian, Luau, Mexican, Oriental, Patriotic, and Western parties. The selection is impressive.

To find the local distributor or get additional information, call the company at 717-532-2131 or send a fax to 1-800-445-2131.

One great addition to any party are life-size cardboard cutouts of movie stars, cartoon characters, and sports figures, available from Advanced Graphics, 941 Garcia Avenue, Pittsburgh, CA 94565-5038, phone, 510-432-2262.

Some choices include: nine versions of Marilyn Monroe, the crew of the starship *Enterprise* (as well as the spaceship!), Frankenstein, Albert Einstein, James Dean, a policeman, Betty Boop, a host of Power Rangers, Batman, the Joker, Betty Grable, Fred Flintstone, Darth Vader, Babe Ruth, and a Wurlitzer Juke Box. Single orders are $25, with prices decreasing with orders of three or more. If you are feeling very rich, Advanced Graphics will create a custom standup or display (maximum size 26 by 73 inches) for $300, with the per standup cost decreasing as the order increases.

Lights

If you are feeling extravagant, buy a string or two of specialty lights (I've seen cacti, pigs, and cows). If these are too pricey for you, but you want to add a little glitz, buy strings of the mini Christmas tree lights in white or another color. Only please, for the sake of your guests, leave the blinker off. Psychedelic went out in the '70s.

Costumes

You can make just about any costume you could imagine by visiting a vintage clothing, thrift, army-navy, joke, or fabric store.

November 30—Dick Clark's Birthday

If the '60s theme is not your thing, November 30 is also a great day for an American Bandstand Party. Poodle skirts and bobbie socks would set the tone for this bash. Serious dancing is a must.

Don't feel overwhelmed by the prospect of creating a costume. Men should consider a flamboyant hat, walking stick, vest, or vintage jacket. A length of shiny black material could make a stunning cloak. Add a hood and scythe and you're Father Time.

Women can create a magnificent "gown" by buying a length of exotic fabric and draping it in a creative fashion. No sewing is needed; just have lots of safety pins on hand. Add a flea market fur piece (preferably one with its head still on) and you're ready for Monte Carlo.

Think creatively about your accessories. Instead of buying costume jewelry, go to a trimmings store and buy a length of faux pearls for about $.50 per yard. Also consider lengths of beads or gold cord. Inexpensive organza or netting is also very versatile for a veil, tutu, or shawl.

I am a sucker for sequins, which come in every conceivable color. The best kind for costumes comes with an elastic backing (in various widths). This can be used for necklaces, bracelets, belts, armbands, headbands, or dress trim. Large rhinestone buttons can be transformed into fabulous diamond rings or pins in a matter of minutes.

When it comes to accessorizing, my personal favorite will always be a boa. Trust me, nothing dresses up an outfit more than a scarlet boa. You can buy one for as little as $10. For $60, you can get a boa "to die for."

If you're into feathers, also consider marabou fluffs, goose coquille, and turkey quills, which can be bought by the bag and glued on to hats, dresses, or fans—or just placed artistically wherever.

For a futuristic look, buy the mesh from which sequins have been cut out. Available at trimmings stores, it's a bargain at $.25 per yard. This flexible metallic "material" would be very drafty for winter nights (after all, it is mostly "holes"), but it would make a great costume for an Extraterrestrial Party.

A visit to the local joke shop is always sure to produce some great ideas. We've found rubber cockroaches, fake scabs, foot-long cigars, and a wonderful pig nose. For traditionalists, there's always the rubber chicken, fake vomit, and Whoopee Cushion.

Remember: The more ludicrous the better. A theme party is no place for understated elegance.

Reference

For a good general guide to period dress, refer to *Harriet Love's Guide to Vintage Chic* (Holt, Rinehart and Winston, 1982). Books on the 1950s, '60s, and '70s will help to inspire you for the Faded Fads, Great Entertainers, or TV parties.

Helpful hint: If your costume involves heavy artillery or rows of bullets across your chest bandit style, don't walk to the party. I made that mistake: ONCE.

Prizes

Specific suggestions are included for each party in the book. There are, however, some general ideas that can be adapted to any party.

CUSTOM BOOKMARKS

This is an inexpensive way to have a theme party favor for all your guests. Pick a favorite expression quote or cartoon. Here are two samples:

> A man's got to make at least one bet every day, else he could be walking around lucky and never know it.
>
> —Jimmy Jones, horse trainer

> You've got to train for rock 'n' roll.
>
> —Mick Jagger

Production is easy. Just pick the size you want (approximately 7 by 2.5 inches), then print your saying either by using a computer or by using rub-on lettering. When you're happy with the result, make a photocopy for each guest. Now you're ready for lamination.

In most areas, local copy stores have laminating machines. The most economical process is to spread out multiple copies of the bookmark on an $8^1/_2$-by-11-inch or 11-by-17-inch sheet of paper. Leave enough for a clear border between the bookmarks for a $^1/_4$-inch border of clear laminate. (You'll get approximately eight bookmarks on an 11-by-17-inch sheet.) Once the sheets are laminated, cut out the individual bookmarks. Lamination should cost between $2.00 and $5.00 per sheet, depending on the desired thickness.

If you can't find a copy store to do your lamination, stationery stores sell clear plastic laminating sheets and you can open up a factory right in your own living room.

MEMO PADS

Custom memo pads with a theme party logo also can be made at the local copy store. Bring in your logo, and you will have your choice of pad sizes. The most practical one probably would be 4.25 by 5.5 inches, so you could make two per $8^1/_2$-by-11-inch sheet of paper. If you're not an Einstein at figuring this out, don't worry. The people at the copy store will help you.

DECEMBER

December 5—Repeal of Prohibition Anniversary

On this day in 1933, the needed thirty-sixth state ratified the repeal of the Eighteenth Amendment to the Constitution. Party on—but leave the car at home!

T-SHIRTS

If you want to go whole hog, you can have custom shirts made up professionally. When we did this, the shirts, printed in one color on 100 percent cotton, cost approximately $5.00 each. Look up local vendors in the Yellow Pages under "T-shirts."

If you want to take a more economical route, make your own. Art supply or party stores sell fabric paints and markers. Selections include squeeze-on dimensional paints, brush-on paints, and glitter paint. All will make it through the wash.

If you want to risk the mess, you might think about having a "make your own T-shirt" activity right at the party. But if your home color scheme is white, I'd think again!

Another option would be to take a walk down memory lane and make your own tie-dye shirts. We did it for a '60s Party and gave out the shirts as prizes for best costume.

NEED HELP?

Look through mail-order catalogs for creative ideas. Here are a few to get you started.

The Klutz Flying Apparatus Catalogue
2121 Staunton Court
Palo Alto, CA 94306
415-424-0739

December 12—Bob Barker's Birthday

Whether you remember him from his early days as host of *Truth or Consequences* or from his singing "Miss America" after the legendary Burt Parks stepped down, Bob Barker (with or without his women problems) remains an American TV legend. Use his birthday for your '60s or '70s TV Party. Alternatively, create your own Game Show Party.

Wireless
Minnesota Public Radio
P.O. Box 64422
St. Paul, MN 55164-0422
1-800-669-9999

M.I.T. Museum Shop Catalogue
265 Massachusetts Avenue
Cambridge, MA 02139
617-253-4462

Time Warner & Sony Sound Exchange
45 N. Industry Court
Deer Park, NY 11729-4614
1-800-521-0042—for CDs, tapes, and music memorabilia

Keep your eye out for publications and games from Ivory Tower Publications, 125 Walnut Street, Watertown, MA 02172 (617-923-1111). Publications include *Dumb Men Jokes, Geriatric Sex Guide,* and *Working Girl's Doodle Book.* PMS/The Bitch Cards are a must for the Politically Incorrect Party.

THOSE EXTRA LITTLE TOUCHES . . .

Some suggestions:

- Take Polaroid photos of everyone at the party. You can either give them to the guests as keepsakes or, if the party is a birthday or going-away party, paste the photos in a "memory book" and have the guests write something next to their pictures. Then present it to the guest of honor.
- Buy several disposable cameras and let your guests snap away all evening. The pictures may not be great, but you may have a potential Annie Leibovitz in the crowd.

HELPFUL HINTS

You don't have to be a rocket scientist to figure out that guests clump like lemmings wherever there is food and drink. So set up the drinks in one room and the food in another. Better yet, have several "food stations" scattered around.

Also, if food is "potluck," with each guest making a contribution, make sure that you're not totally dependent on one person for a major portion of the meal. Some will come fashionably late, and some might not arrive at all. So have a critical mass of food set out before any guests arrive. And have a reserve of beer, wine, and soft drinks, just in case. No one ever complains if there's too much, but if there isn't enough . . .

MUSIC YOU CAN'T RESIST

Ultimately, any party will be a success if the guests "get down" and boogie. Our experience is that the best dancing music is a "mix and match" of artists. It is rare to have an entire CD or tape that has one great dancing song after another.

For our bigger and more elaborate parties, we have indulged ourselves by hiring a disc jockey (affordable if several friends share the expense). While the DJ adds a lot to the party, it is an extravagance that isn't necessary for a great soiree. The most practical route—and the one we take for just about every party we give—is to make our own ninety-minute "dancing tapes" and have a fair number of classic rock-and-roll tapes or compact discs on hand.

As baby boomers, nothing gets us up and dancing like a great selection of 1950s, '60s, and '70s music. If this is also your orientation, here's a sample of ninety minutes of music.

Side 1

"Proud Mary" by Tina Turner—"Some people like to do things nice and easy, we like to do them nice and rough." Don't we know, Tina.

"Heat Wave" by Martha Reeves and the Vandellas

"Needles and Pins" by The Searchers

"In the Summertime" by Mungo Jerry

"You're Going to Lose that Girl" by The Beatles

"Honky Tonk Woman" by The Rolling Stones

"Barbara Ann" by The Beach Boys

"Runaround Sue" by Dion

"Soldier Boy" by The Shirelles
"Twist" by Chubby Checker
"Come Go with Me" by The Del-Vikings
"Wonderful World" by Sam Cooke
"The Stroll" by The Diamonds
"At the Hop" by Danny and the Juniors
"Peppermint Twist" by Joey Dee & the Starliters
"Sea Cruise" by Frankie Ford
"Blue Suede Shoes" by Elvis Presley
"I'm Walking" by Fats Domino
"I Get Around" by The Beach Boys

Side 2

"That'll Be the Day" by Buddy Holly & The Crickets
"Come Softly to Me" by The Fleetwoods
"Breaking Up Is Hard to Do" by Neil Sedaka
"Roll Over Beethoven" by The Beatles
"Rock Around the Clock" by Bill Haley
"Get Off My Cloud" by The Rolling Stones
"All Shook Up" by Elvis Presley
"Tenth Avenue Freezeout" by Bruce Springsteen
"Respect" by Aretha Franklin
"(Sittin' on the) Dock of the Bay" by Otis Redding
"Rock and Roll Music" by The Beatles
"Rescue Me" by Fontella Bass
"Peggy Sue" by Buddy Holly & The Crickets
"Love Potion #9" by The Searchers
"Johnny B. Goode" by Chuck Berry
"Bad Moon Rising" by Creedence Clearwater Revival
"Blue Moon" by The Marcels
"Tequila" by The Champs
"Goodnight, Sweetheart, Goodnight" by The Spaniels

THE EASY ROUTE

The music industry has already put together some fantastic anthologies for just about every kind of music you could imagine.
Some possibilities are:

Billboard Top Rock & Roll Hits (every year from 1955 through the 1980s)
The Cruisin' Years (Rykodisc)
41 Original Hits from American Graffiti (MCA)

And a sure winner would be any of the CDs/tapes from Warner's Baby Boomer Classics series:

Dance Seventies	*Psychedelic Sixties*
Dance Sixties	*Rockin' Seventies*
Electric Sixties	*Soul Sixties*
Groovin' Sixties	*Surfin' Sixties*

If you can find these old classic LP collections, they would be wonderful to have:

Top 100 Rock 'n' Roll Hits (five-album set from RCA)
The Greatest Rock 'n' Roll Hits (five-album set from Roulette Records)
At the Hop (two-album set from ABC Records)
The Soul Years (a twenty-fifth anniversary special album from Atlantic)

So put on your dancing shoes, roll up the rug, and let those feet fly. There is always ibuprofen in the morning!

SUGGESTED READINGS FOR EVEN BETTER PARTIES

*

General Interest: Music and Pop Culture

Billboard Top 1000 Singles: 1955–1990, compiled by Joel Whitburn (Hal Leonard, 1991)

The Pop Sixties: A Personal and Irreverent Guide by Andrew J. Edelstein (World Almanac, 1985)

Popular Culture: The Great Contemporary Issue Series, Set 1, vol. 9, David Manning White, advisory editor (Arno Press, 1978)

The Seventies: From Hot Pants to Hot Tubs by Andrew J. Edelstein and Kevin McDonough (Dutton, 1990)

Sixties Going on Seventies by Nora Sayre (Arbor House, 1973)

The Sixties: The Art, Attitudes, Politics, and Media of our Most Explosive Decade, edited by Gerald Howard (Marlowe & Company, 1995)

Wagons Ho

The American West by Dee Brown (Charles Scribner's Sons, 1994)

The Encyclopedia of Western Lawmen and Outlaws by Jay Robert Nash (Da Capo Press, 1994)

The Great West by David Lavender (Houghton Mifflin Company, 1965)

The Home Book of Western Humor, edited by Phillip Ault (Dodd Mead & Company, 1967)

The Oxford Dictionary of the American West, edited by Clyde A. Milner II, Carol A. O'Connor, Martha A. Sandweiss (Oxford University Press, 1994)

Way Out West by Jane and Michael Stern (HarperCollins, 1993)

Speakeasy

Ain't We Got Fun: Essays, Lyrics, and Stories of the Twenties, edited by Barbara H. Solomon (New American Library, 1980)

The Bootleggers and Their Era by Kenneth Allsop (Doubleday, 1961)

The Twenties: Fords, Flappers & Fanatics by George E. Mowry (Prentice-Hall, 1963)

You Must Remember This: An Oral History of Manhattan From the 1890s to World War II by Jeff Kisseloff (Schocken Books, 1989)

Politically Incorrect

The Encyclopedia of Bad Taste by Jane and Michael Stern (Harper Perennial, 1990)

The Official Politically Correct Dictionary and Handbook by Henry Beard and Christopher Cerf (Villard, 1993)

Private Parts by Howard Stern (Simon & Schuster, 1993)

Faded Fads

American Fads: From Silly Putty and Swallowing Goldfish to Hot Pants and Hula Hoops by Richard A. Johnson (Beech Tree, 1985)

Fads: America's Crazes, Fevers, and Fancies from the 1890s to the 1970s by Peter Skolnik, with Laura Torbet and Nikki Smith (Thomas Y. Crowell, 1978)

Fads, Follies, and Delusions of the American People by Paul Sann (Bonanza, 1967)

Panati's Parade of Fads, Follies, and Manias by Charles Panati (Harper Perennial, 1991)

Great Entertainers

Rock Movers and Shakers: An A to Z of the People Who Made Rock Happen, compiled by Dafydd Rees and Luke Crampton (Banson Marketing Ltd, 1989)

That Old Time Rock & Roll: A Chronicle of an Era by Richard Aquila (Schirmer Books, 1989)

The Billboard Book of American Singing Groups: A History 1940–1990 by Jay Warner (Billboard Books, 1992)

The Billboard Book of Top 40 Hits, compiled by Joel Whitburn (Billboard Books, 1992)

The Ultimate Encyclopedia of Rock, edited by Michael Heatley (Harper Perennial, 1993)

Nerds

The Computer Insectiary: A Field Guide to Viruses, Bugs, Worms, Trojan Horses, and Other Stuff that Will Eat Your Programs and Rot Your Brain by Roger Ebert and John Kratz (Andrew & McMeel, 1994)

Watergate

All the President's Men by Carl Bernstein and Bob Woodward (Simon & Schuster, 1974)

Behind the Lines: Cartoons by Tony Auth by Tony Auth (Houghton Mifflin, 1977)

Big Brother and the Holding Company: The World Behind Watergate, edited by Steve Weissman (Ramparts Press, 1974)

Blind Ambition by John Dean (Simon & Schuster, 1976)

The Final Days by Bob Woodward and Carl Bernstein (Simon & Schuster, 1976)

The Fireside Watergate by Nicholas von Hoffman and Garry Trudeau (Sheed & Ward, 1973)

The Haldeman Diaries: Inside the Nixon White House by H. R. Haldeman (Berkley Books, 1995)

The King & Us (editorial cartoons) by Paul Conrad (Clymer Publications, 1974)

The Stonewall: The Real Story of the Watergate Prosecution by Richard Ben-Veniste and George Frampton, Jr. (Simon & Schuster, 1977)

The Women of Watergate by Madeleine Edmondson and Alden Duer Cohen (Stein and Day, 1975)

Scandals

Fall From Grace: Sex, Scandal, and Corruption in American Politics from 1702 to the Present by Shelly Ross (Ballantine, 1988)

O.J.'s Legal Pad, fabricated by Henry Beard and John Boswell (Villard Books, 1995)

Scandals Annual 1993: Who Got Caught Doing What in 1992 by The Paragon Project (St. Martin's Press, 1993)*

They Walked a Crooked Mile: An Account of the Greatest Scandals, Swindlers, and Outrages of All Time by Charles Franklin (Hard, 1967)

The Kennedy Scandals and Tragedies by Ann James (Publications International, Ltd, 1991)

'50s/'60s/'70s TV

Bad TV: The Very Best of the Very Worst by Craig Nelson (Delta, 1995)

Total Television by Alex McNeil (Penguin, 1980, revised 1991)

The TV Almanac by Louise Phillips and Burnham Holmes (Macmillan, 1994)

The TV Encyclopedia by David Inman (Perigee Books, 1991)

TV Game Shows by Maxine Fabe (Dolphin, 1979)

The TV Guide TV Book by Ed Weiner and Editors of TV Guide (Harper Perennial, 1992)

TV Theme Song Sing-Along Book by John Javna (St. Martin's Press, 1984)

TV Trivia Teasers by W. Wilson Casey (Popular Culture, 1984)

*Note: *The Scandals Annual* has not been updated for more recent years.

Cold War

The Fifties by David Halberstam (Villard, 1993)
In the Eye of the Storm: Castro, Khrushchev, Kennedy and the Missile Crisis by Carlos Lechuga (Ocean Press, 1995)

Cold War

The Fifties by David Halberstam (Villard, 1993).

Inside the Cuban Missile Crisis edited by ... Ocean Press, 1999.

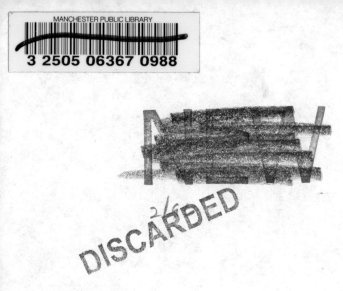